MW01235418

Would Jesus Discriminate?

THE 21ST CENTURY QUESTION

Rev. Dr. Cindi Love

ISBN: 978-1-4251-7288-6

*We at Trafford believe that it is the responsibility of us all, as both individuals
and corporations, to make choices that are environmentally and socially sound.
You, in turn, are supporting this responsible conduct each time you purchase a
Trafford book, or make use of our publishing services. To find out how you are
helping, please visit www.trafford.com/responsiblepublishing.html*

*Our mission is to efficiently provide the world's finest, most comprehensive
book publishing service, enabling every author to experience success.
To find out how to publish your book, your way, and have it available
worldwide, visit us online at www.trafford.com/10510*

 www.trafford.com

North America & international
toll-free: 1 888 232 4444 (USA & Canada)
phone: 250 383 6864 ♦ fax: 250 383 6804 ♦ email: info@trafford.com

The United Kingdom & Europe
phone: +44 (0)1865 722 113 ♦ local rate: 0845 230 9601
facsimile: +44 (0)1865 722 868 ♦ email: info.uk@trafford.com

10 9 8 7 6 5 4 3 2 1

To Patrick Leo Herndon, my brother;
Thank you for being so authentic in a world
that did not honor you.
You gave me a chance to get it right this time.
I won't fail you again.

Table of Contents

Acknowledgements

I want to honor and thank the people in my life who call the questions that matter into my consciousness—firstly, my beloved spouse of 27 years, Sue Jennings. For better, for worse, richer or poorer, in sickness and in health, you have stood with me and loved me. And secondly, the "next generation"—my amazing children Hannah and Joshua, my precious daughter-in-law, Melanie, and my son's much-loved partner, Mark. Without you I would often persist in behaviors that are not helpful, not loving and not true to my real belief that God so Loved the World—all of us! Thank you my dear family for caring enough about me to confront me and love me through good times and bad. Thank you, Gina, Christopher and Russell for your love and faith in me. Thank you to my family of choice – Alan, Ritchie, Bill, Brian, Christy, Cathy, Sherry, Boes, Rob and Sarah, Van and David, Sissy, Linda and Steve.

I also want to thank the incredible leaders, members, friends, lay leaders and clergy of Metropolitan Community Churches worldwide. You reflect the whole heart of God in the very fact that you exist and that you persist in offering a Table that is always open to everyone. I love you and need you and thank you for your love and support of our community, of my family and of me.

I particularly want to lift up the name of Rev. Margaret Walker who told me that I was called to ministry and would not leave me alone until I really listened. Thank you, Rev. Carolyn Mobley, for believing that I could "fill your shoes" during your sabbatical and for letting me try.

Thank you, Rev. Dwayne Johnson for trusting Rev. Carolyn's judgment and trusting me with your community. Without that experience, I would not be a minister today. Thank you, good people of Resurrection and Exodus Metropolitan Community Churches in Houston and Abilene, Texas, respectively, for allowing me to serve you as a student pastor. You were (and are) patient and loving and a blessing that overflows in my life.

Thank you, Rev. Elder Troy Perry, Founder and First Moderator of Metropolitan Community Churches for believing in me, praying for me and holding fast to your belief that God loves us all. Thank you, Rev. Elder Don Eastman, Vice-Moderator of MCC and long time pastor of the first church I was called to pastor. You are Elder Statesperson in my life and I count on your wisdom and love every day.

Thank you, Rev. Elder Nancy Wilson, Moderator of MCC for making me part of your Tribe. I cannot image life without your leadership, faith and love. Thank you, Rev. Elder Lillie Brock for believing I could lead MCC of Greater Dallas when it was yet a Journey of the Heart and for being my friend through it all.

Thank you Rev. Elder Jim Mitulski for loving me, for stretching my heart and mind to places I did not know existed, and thank you for mentoring my son. Thank you, Rev. Elder Ken Martin for your quiet, loving, all-accepting heart.

Thank you, Rev. Elder Darlene Garner, for you are also Elder Statesperson to me and I look to you for the deep roots. Thank you, Rev. Elder Arlene Ackerman for making the youth of MCC so visible to me, for being a great mom and an amazing pastor of your community. Thank you, Rev. Elder Glenna Shepherd for your love and faithfulness through every trial with me.

Thank you, Rev. Elder Diane Fisher for always calling the oppressed into the room with us and for making us see their faces and hear their voices. Thank you, Marvin Bagwell, Barbara Crabtree, Stephen Harte, Julie Krueger, Rev. Jeff Miner, John Vespa, and Marsha Warren for being courageous enough to hire me and stick with me.

Thank you to the FOCs. You know who you are and why you are called FOCs and I love you. Thank you, *Team That Beats With One Heart*—Kathy Beasley, Rev. Sharon Bezner, Rev.Jim Birkitt, Florin Buhucheanu, Franklin Calvin, Angel Collie, Judy Dale, Rev. Deb Dysert, Rev. Karla Fleshman, Rev. Thomas Friedhoff, Vickey Gibbs, Rev. Jennifer Glass, Rev. Robert Griffin, Rev. Hector Gutierrez, Tessa Lee, Steve Marlowe, Connie Meadows, Valarie Parson, Stedney Phillips, Rev. Gelson Piber, Joseph Rattan, Rev. Elder Nori Rost, Enrique Zenteño, and Frank Zerilli.

Thank you, Leah Sloan, for your patient and capable editing. Any errors or omissions are my own.

Most of all, thank you, Jesus, for showing me the way.

Introduction

Barbara Delaney

Congratulations on your choice of *Would Jesus Discriminate? The 21st Century Question*. I had the distinct pleasure of attending the first Town Hall Meeting for the Campaign in the spring of 2006. While there, I met Rev. Dr. Jeff Miner, the Senior Pastor of Jesus Metropolitan Community Church in Indianapolis. I also met the author of this book, the woman who developed the concept for the campaign, Rev. Dr. Cindi Love.

Before she was ordained in 2003, Cindi was an educator, an entrepreneur and corporate executive. The first company she founded became #73 on the INC 500 Fastest Growing Private Businesses in North America in 1990. MIT and the Young Entrepreneur's Organization named her one of the top 50 entrepreneurs in North America in 1990 as part of the *Birthing of Giants* program (www.yeo.com).

She founded one of the largest Apple computer sales agencies in the United States and another company that she sold to The TORO Company (NYSE:TTC) in 1996. In 1999, she went to work as the Chief Operating Officer in North America for an Israeli high technology firm. This position propelled her into yet another new experience, a private venture capital placement with some of the largest investment houses in the United States and the U.K.

She left corporate America in 2003 and reentered the education field as Executive Dean of Brookhaven College in Dallas, Texas. While leading the Corporate & Continuing Education Division at the college, she completed the requirements for ordination with Metropolitan Community Church.

Now, in addition to her role as the chief executive officer of Metropolitan Community Churches worldwide, she serves as one of the leading religious voices on the Human Rights Campaign Faith and Religion Council in Washington, D.C. She also serves as an advocate for adults who are chronically disabled and, when time permits, serves as guest preacher for churches. Her favorite sermon title? You guessed it! "Would Jesus Discriminate?"

Ask her what her greatest achievement has been and she will say, "I have three. Discovering my relationship to the Holy; giving birth to Joshua and Hannah, now ages 33 and 30, respectively; and marrying Sue, my life-partner of 27 years."

Dr. Love says the *Would Jesus Discriminate? Campaign* is an important exercise for both Christians and non-Christians and the citizens of the United States. Why? Because religious based bigotry is the leading cause of endemic discrimination and the inevitable outcome thereof, violence.

Dr. Love asserts that the Christian Church is teaching some things that Jesus never taught, particularly regarding homosexuals.

She asks readers to consider, "What if the dominant philosophy regarding the issue of gay people in society and our churches is wrong? What if homosexuals were offered *full* citizenship: life, liberty and the pursuit of happiness? How might our country improve if an estimated ten percent of our best and brightest people (not to mention a roughly equal proportion of the rest of us) were not arbitrarily oppressed?"

Regardless of your religious beliefs about homosexuality or your personal preferences about homosexuals as neighbors, you'll find her analysis provocative. Asking the question, "Would Jesus discriminate?" is a simple way to start a meaningful dialogue with your family, co-workers and your church about the future of America today.

Martina Navratilova, Honorary Chair for Metropolitan Community Churches Global Conference for 2006-2007, likes to tell people to "get in the game." The *Would Jesus Discriminate? Campaign* is playing for serious stakes. The quality of life of millions of people depends on our individual willingness to confront discrimination each and every time we see it or experience it. Thank you, Cindi, for sticking your neck out on this one.

Barbara Delaney, CEO
Navratilova, Inc.
www.rainbowcard.com
www.martinanavratilova.com

Thank you for choosing to read *Would Jesus Discriminate? The 21st Century Question.* As a former executive in a 100+ year old publicly traded company (The TORO Company) and an entrepreneur at heart, I love to tell the story of this dynamic community engagement and marketing campaign. The test launch and subsequent phases were led by Rev. Dr. Jeff Miner, Harvard-attorney-turned-pastor, and the members of his church, Jesus Metropolitan Community Church (MCC) in Indianapolis.[1]

Rev. Dr. Jeff's congregants in Indianapolis were supported by a very bold and committed financial partner, Mitchell Gold, the founder of Faith in America[2] (FIA) as well as the denomination where I serve as CEO, Metropolitan Community Churches[3]

(MCC). I am deeply grateful to Rev. Jeff and his congregation, to Mitchell and his business partner, Bob Williams, as well as Jimmy Creech, the Executive Director of FIA. They took a big risk and this book tells the story of their commitment as well as the path that brought me to the development of the concept and its ultimate launch in the marketplace.

The campaign is an excellent reflection of Margaret Mead's assertion that a few committed people have the power to change the world,[4] and this book details, for the benefit of those of you who are "marketing geeks" like me, a highly practical and successful application of the theories of market innovation and community engagement proposed by Everett Rogers[5] and Frank Bass.[6] The first phase of the campaign produced a *16 percent shift* in consumer attitudes in Indianapolis as reported by Public Policy Polling, Raleigh, North Carolina.[7]

When I was in corporate America, I would have given my eye teeth to produce that kind of result in a test phase of a product launch. In industry, we had millions of dollars at our disposal and the best marketing firms in the country to guide us. Clearly, Rev. Dr. Jeff and the people at Jesus MCC had something better. I think those of us in the marketing industry can learn a lot from their experiences.

If you are a member of the Christian Right[8] and/or a practicing homophobe, this book asks you to evaluate the destructiveness to our American society of heterosexism and discrimination against non-heterosexual people. If you are a person of faith who identifies as Lesbian, Gay, Bisexual, Transgender, Gender Queer, Homosexual, Questioning or Intersex (In the interest of brevity and readability, the term non-heterosexual will hereafter be used in reference to individuals who so identify.) this book calls you "out of the closet" and into a *Would Jesus Discriminate?* t-shirt. You, among all the people on this planet, are some of the best-equipped ambassadors for this campaign because you already know how to take great risks for the sake of truth; and most of you, with the patience of Job, will deny neither God nor your own integrity.[9]

I know, some will think it a great irony, (if not a blasphemy!) to speak of non-heterosexual people as ambassadors for anything with the name "Jesus" in it. But I believe it is God's truth. The Bible is full of stories in which people perceived as unlikely, perhaps even unsuitable, candidates were chosen to fulfill God's purposes, and those individuals proved surprisingly faithful to the call.

When it came time to implement the *Would Jesus Discriminate? Campaign*, we looked for some "unlikely, yet faithful people" in a place that no one would consider a marketing Mecca—Indianapolis, epitome of the Midwest. We were lucky and blessed to have chosen Jesus MCC.

Though the campaign is low-budget, it has proven to be high-impact in terms of increasing awareness and changing attitudes, and I have no doubt that the results in Minneapolis and Dallas and other campaign locations throughout the world will be comparable to the significantly positive outcomes achieved in Indianapolis.

But perhaps more importantly, the campaigns will re-sound the prophet Jeremiah's timeless call to "Administer justice every morning; rescue from the hand of his oppressor the one who has been robbed."[10] Jeremiah's exhortation was particularly urgent in the 1940s when the Nazi party controlled much of Europe and "it wasn't helpful to express sympathy for hunted persons or even to pray for them in their terminal misery. Action had to be the order of the day, however inconvenient or dangerous."[11] And the prophet's words resonate strongly in today's climate too, as we see people robbed of the right to live with dignity and full citizenship—or even robbed of life itself as in the cases of Matthew Shepard and Sean Kennedy.[12]

In that earlier time Christians, Muslims and agnostics risked their lives to save Jews from the terror that became the Holocaust. They hid them in their homes, ferried them through secret tunnels and, in some cases, paid the ultimate penalty for taking those risks. The Jews call the people who engaged in that singular effort the "Righteous Among Nations." I believe that such people live in the US and throughout the world today, and that these otherwise ordinary people will step forward to help save the lives and dignity of non-heterosexual people as well.

Early in 2005, I presented the concept for this campaign to several potential funding sources and I met with resistance. The idea was considered "too inflammatory" by most of them and, as time did tell, the campaign really pushed some buttons. The reactions of religious members of the Christian Right have been particularly noteworthy. Any marketer loves it when an ad provokes a strong reaction. Let me share a message we received recently:

> Hi. I am praying for you people. I think it's a very sad day in this world which is what this world is coming to, the false society showing, billboards promoting gays and then bringing the Christian amateur to it. You obviously do not read the Bible through God's eyes, through a child's eyes, through anyone's eyes you can read where those statements, you guys have misconstrued. I mean, I don't even see how you even came up with anything about being gay out of the word of the Bible.

> I have a huge list of verses I would be more than happy to fax you stating that homosexuality is a sin in the Bible. We don't uphold murders, you know, and you know it's a sin, and, God has said that, Jesus has said it's a sin and I really feel bad for you people and I will definitely pray for you people who promote this awfulness. You know all this does is it does make people read the Bible though

and what you're saying on these billboards is plainly not true when you read the Scripture especially about Ruth and Naomi. I mean, actually it's getting people probably to read the Bible who normally don't and see that what you're saying is absolutely wrong. I don't see how you come up with what you come up with. It doesn't even state that whatsoever.

So, I pray for you and hope that you come around and see how Jesus really believes and hope that you will follow him and not the other way. Thank you.[13]

In addition to this type of reaction, we are seeing a strong response by bloggers, whose impact on market perception is a new key indicator for those who study such phenomena.[14] Significant numbers of bloggers are posting pictures of all the campaign billboards and many of their postings include links to the Would Jesus Discriminate website (www.wouldjesusdiscriminate.com) and/or Jesus MCC's website.

Rev. Jim Birkitt, Director of Public Relations for Metropolitan Community Churches has been tracking content in mainstream as well as alternative media outlets. The following summaries are a mere sampling of the intensely moving and powerful records that people are creating:

- An agnostic transwoman writes of being moved to tears as she visited the website wouldjesusdiscriminate.com and listened to the on-line sermon.
- Gay people write of being hurt by organized religion but feeling proud that the Indianapolis church is taking a stand and putting out a different message.
- A gay man writes that he's had little use for organized religion in his own life, but he'd gladly wear a "Would Jesus Discriminate?" t-shirt.

- A man begins his blog with: "Finally, a website we can send our grandmas to."
- A blogger, neither sexual nor gender orientation specified, writes: "I just found this website which I am *completely* in love with: wouldjesusdiscriminate.com. It's amazing. Go there."

Rev. Birkitt says:

> We don't yet know how to measure the impact of these blogs, but there's a whole new level of response to the campaign that goes beyond the already very significant reaction to the billboards, newspaper ads, yard signs, bumper stickers and t-shirts. It feels to me like something very pivotal is happening related to communications strategy and blogging right now... Some of the blogs have counters and show 8,000 or even 17,000 readers.
>
> I am fascinated by the whole grassroots-alternative-media-viral-nature of blogging, and how it's taking the current campaign to people beyond the city limits of Indianapolis, and beyond the state lines of Indiana. And I do think that this campaign has all the potential to break into the wider, broader public consciousness in the sense of perhaps being a national movement, or with large numbers of people in diverse places "getting" the message and passing it on.

I think Rev. Jim is right, so this book is my way of "passing it on" to people just like you—moms, co-workers, church-goers, neighbors. *This book is mostly for you, my fellow Americans. We are strong but we are wrong and it is time to step forward and do something about it. The world is following our example.*

P.S. Image files for t-shirts, bumper stickers, yard signs and billboards can be customized (name and website) and provided at no cost to individuals, churches and other organizations who want to stage a campaign. If you are interested, just call 1-866-HOPEMCC. (1-866-467-3611)

Don't Confuse Bigotry
against gays and lesbians
with Religious Truth.
WouldJesusDiscriminate.com

1

Who Moved My Jesus?

While I was working in "Corporate America" from 1981 to 2003, I consumed a steady diet of business books. One short read that influenced me was *Who Moved My Cheese?* by Spencer Johnson, M.D.[15] Dr. Johnson's website[16] says that he created the story to help himself deal with a difficult change in his life. His life did indeed become better, and more than three million people bought his book, too.

Dr. Johnson has said that it is not his story that helps people, but instead that the benefit lies in the way people interpret and apply the work to their own situations.[17] I hope *Would Jesus Discriminate?* can serve you in a similar way. I believe that the story of this campaign is an excellent case study for marketing and sales professionals, community organizers, sociologists, professional clergy and politicians. I also believe that its most significant impact will be in the lives of people who read the story honestly ask themselves, "*Would* Jesus discriminate?" and then extend themselves to the more telling question, "Do I?"

Like Dr. Spencer Johnson, I have written, in part at least, to help myself. I believe that the members of the Christian Right *moved my Jesus* and this book is my way of taking Him back. They started moving Him when I entered Sunday School and by the time I was baptized, I believed that I, along with millions of other sinners, was personally responsible for putting Christ on the Cross of Calvary. Now, if you have not experienced the fundamentalist outlook, that idea may seem nonsensical, but trust me, that is what I thought.

Without my being aware of the process, my teachers and role models had *moved my Jesus,* and indeed had helped me to move Him well beyond the scope of the children's song "Jesus Loves Me." Adopting personal guilt for the crucifixion wasn't the only way I co-opted Jesus either.

I believed Jesus "loved the little children" but the only children I knew were white. In fact, the only church people I knew were white, and so I internalized the idea that salvation was a pretty exclusive deal. Of course, I knew that my job was to tell the Good News (A sign posted inside the church building read "Untold thousands are dying everyday untold." I felt guilty every time I read it.) but in my youthful zeal, I interpreted the Bible literally, spoke unwittingly from a position of privilege, and unconsciously maintained walls between myself and others—all while working to bring those others "into the fold."

Until 1964, the public schools and churches in my hometown were not racially integrated and I saw nothing wrong with that. Until 1981, prejudice allowed me to justify the exclusion of all women, myself as well, from positions of leadership in the church. And, until 1996, prejudice allowed me to justify the barring of non-heterosexual persons from the Body of Christ—and again, I effectively excluded myself.

The ragged edge of our communities, to which non-heterosexual people are relegated by members of the Christian Right, is a place created by patriarchy and hedged about by racism, sexism, and heterosexism. It is the same silent closet into which society and the church have often shut women. It is the same shame-filled space to which Americans once consciously consigned people of African descent.

I submit that we have a responsibility as human beings to defend the lives and dignity of the oppressed. Our silence shames us and is deadly in its lethargic responses to the injustices suffered by non-heterosexual people. We must step up and speak out.

This "stepping forward" is particularly important for all of us who claim the name "Christian," else we will surely hear "…just as you did not do it to one of the least of these, you did not do it to me."[18] I submit that patriarchy fundamentally desecrates the central message of the life and ministry of Jesus, and it is our particular responsibility, as those who claim to imitate the life and love of Jesus Christ, to "reset" the oppression that patriarchy engenders.

It is my hope that you will find your way to stand beside me. Let me ask you, "What do *you* think? *Would Jesus discriminate?*" You don't have to be a Christian or even be religious to answer the questions.

My hypothesis is that Jesus would not and did not discriminate against homosexuals, and the fact that Jesus never mentioned homosexuality at all supports, I believe, that hypothesis. I think Jesus would treat homosexuals exactly the same as he did women and non-Jews—lovingly, graciously and inclusively. So, if our current leaders want to be followers of Jesus Christ, and many profess that they do, they face a significant task. As do those of us who elect them.

Bishop Carlton Pearson says:

> The most ghastly irony in Christianity today is the preponderance of leaders who espouse hatred, prejudice, terrorism, arrogance, ignorance and oppression while claiming all the while to be true Christians. There is a difference in being a follower and being a disciple of Jesus. A follower is a person who accepts the religion built around His teachings. A disciple is a student of Jesus, who reflects His Spirit and walks in His teachings in daily life. A true disciple is like Him in word and in deed. He or she will abandon sick, abusive religion and move on, as Jesus did, into more spiritually relevant realities.[19]

I had to abandon the religious affiliation of my childhood so that I could move on into a more spiritually relevant reality. I believe that most members of the Christian Right would make the same move if they spent more time considering the question "Would Jesus discriminate?" instead of limiting their intellectual exposure to a steady stream of unilateral, ultraconservative rhetoric.

It is hard to think for yourself when the presumed moral authorities have already judged between good and bad on your behalf, and have, for your convenience, compressed "right thinking" into sound bites that bombard you from every imaginable source. Under those conditions it's incredibly difficult to change your mind or to draw conclusions contrary to the accepted wisdom of the pervasive culture.

Walter Bagehot said, in his book *Physics and Politics*:

> One of the greatest pains to human nature is the pain of a new idea. It... makes you think that after all, your

favorite notions may be wrong, your firmest beliefs ill-
founded...Naturally therefore; common men hate a
new idea, and are disposed more or less to ill-treat the
original man who brings it.[20]

I had to change the way I thought about my faith in Jesus and that
wasn't easy, for it meant I was no longer at home in the church of
my childhood, a place that had been precious to me. That church
was familiar and comfortable, but I had to leave it behind, because
it was also excluding and discriminating.

I started thinking differently about Jesus when I divorced. My
church certainly treated me differently. My comfort zone shifted
and I felt defensive, less included and more "suspect." During that
time, I thought about what Jesus did while He was walking the earth
and what seemed important to him. After all, he reached out to a
woman who was not merely divorced, but an adulteress as well.

I paid much closer attention to what the Bible really said after my
divorce. I paid more attention to Jesus' choices. The more I studied
the man Jesus, the more I realized what a radical He was and I grew
to like Him. I suppose I had always loved Him but in a very distant
way because he was "too good" for me (a woman and a sinner).

The Jesus I discovered in my free state of being (no church to go
to) was a very cool guy. He surrounded Himself with individuals
who were despised and rejected by the authorities of the day. He
appeared to really love and respect women and children. In *What
Jesus Meant*, noted historian Garry Wills says,

He [Jesus] walks through social barriers and taboos as if
they were cobwebs. People and practices other men were
required to shun he embraces with an equanimity that
infuriates the proper and observant of his culture.[21]

What a gift and a legacy Jesus gave to those of us who long for
integrity in our culture and communities—infuriating the proper

and observant with love and truth. Ask yourself again as you think about the wonderful image of Jesus that Wills has given us—*Would Jesus discriminate? Do I?*

REV. DR. CINDI LOVE

2

Corrupting the Message of Jesus

I contend that the Christian church (And remember, I belong to a Christian church; in fact, I help run a Christian denomination) has corrupted the message of Jesus and has actually lied about what He really said. Yes, I know these are strong words—in my West Texas hometown people would call them "fightin' words"—but I believe them with all of my heart and intellect and, therefore, cannot state otherwise.

The traditional Christian church has so much invested in excluding "the other" that it has forgotten its call to do justice, practice mercy and walk humbly with God.[22] I was a part of that traditional church for many years and I made major contributions to the perpetuation of the lie that Jesus discriminated, especially against non-heterosexuals. I was part of the Christian Right and I was dead wrong.

In *Perfect Enemies: The Members of the Christian Right, the Gay Movement, and the Politics of the 1990s*, Chris Bull and John Gallagher explain that discrimination, in particular discrimination against gays, is a core feature of the Christian Right's agenda:

> Ultimately, the members of the Christian Right's antigay crusade boils down to reasserting the right not to associate with homosexuals in diverse areas of American life, from the military to the workplace, a right they do not apply nor dare advocate with regard to any other minority group. Such reckless arguments, going far beyond recognizing the right of religious people to make up their minds on matters of morality, improperly establish discrimination as a theological imperative, thus rendering gay activists' suspicion of religious arguments in public policy all the more well-founded and driving the wedge between the groups still deeper.[23]

Indeed, today's religious landscape is sculpted, in part, by the anti-gay messages and strategies of groups such as Focus on the Family and the American Family Association. In addition, the Institute for Religion & Democracy promotes divisive strategies such as pitting people of color against non-heterosexual people—including groups in Latin America, Africa and Asia.

It is also true that specifically anti-gay groups raise and spend a significantly greater amount for promoting their issues in the media. The four largest anti-gay groups outstrip their "opponents" collections by about 4 to 1; the four largest non-heterosexual advocacy groups spend about 40 million yearly educating the public about their issues, while the Right spends nearly 190 million each year on the same activities.[24]

The Christian Right, through its media success, has positioned itself as the "voice of reason" or "family/faith voice." Most Americans do not read the Bible for themselves,[25] but rely instead on their own clergy, church leaders or popular religious figures for interpretation of Scripture and other sacred texts. These facts, coupled with the Christian Right's recent leveraging of its financial base to achieve dominance of most media outlets in the United States, do not encourage people to stand in solidarity with non-heterosexual people.

Indeed, to do so is to invite rejection from peers and co-workers, family members and/or religious authorities. Such would be a heavy price for the average individual, churchgoer or no, to pay. In spite of all that though, I believe in people's basic goodness and also in their ability to judge fairly when they're really "tuned in," and this book is my attempt to *turn up the volume*.

When I developed the concept for the campaign, I had a lot of ideas, but a simple goal: I wanted neighbors to ask neighbors the question "Would Jesus discriminate?" and then talk to each other about what they really thought. I wanted to open up dialogue between members of the Christian Right and non-heterosexuals as well as between members of the Christian Right and progressive heterosexuals. I didn't actually think about people starting to read the Bible more as a result of the Campaign, but that has proven to be a collateral benefit.

In addition to my goal of stimulating dialogue, I wanted to increase the number of opportunities for hetero- and non-heterosexual people of faith to encounter each other. I remain convinced that the more these individuals interact on the basis of their faith, the more rapidly bigotry based on religion will decrease. My picture of heaven on earth comprises a juxtaposition of the vision of Rev. Dr. Martin Luther King Jr.[26] with Will Rogers' famous line, "I've never met a man I didn't like."[27] I dream of the day when people, whether straight or gay, and regardless of their religious affiliations, can meet at the local Starbucks to strategize about their next joint project to feed the poor, shelter the homeless and/or minister to people living with HIV/AIDS.

The *Would Jesus Discriminate? Campaign* was conceived during a time of introspection when I had to ask myself "Do I discriminate?" and now I am inviting you to walk that same path and consider that same question. If you have the same answers and end up in the same place I did, you'll want to get your own t-shirt or bumper sticker because you won't be able to go back "in the closet" about the truth of discrimination in America once you've "come out" to yourself. Don't be afraid. There are lots of other people willing to stand beside you once they know that you're ready to stand up for the truth. Most of us want to live in a safe, peaceful and just America. I don't think this world can ever be its best until the people who have problems with one another are the people talking to each other. It is easy to hate or fear someone you don't really know. So, get out there and ask your neighbors what they think about the 21st Century Question—*Would Jesus discriminate?* I think you'll discover that it's the best neighborhood improvement project you've experienced in a long time.

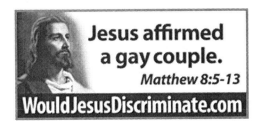

REV. DR. CINDI LOVE

3

Diffusion of Innovation Model

When I was in corporate America, I had the good fortune to test several marketing theories (see Appendix I), so when it came time to select a basis for the *Would Jesus Discriminate? Campaign,* I already had some working knowledge. I opted to apply Rogers' five-stage model for the diffusion of innovation and, as evidenced by the 16 percent increase in positive attitudes towards non-heterosexual people, it worked!

This chapter provides an overview of the theory underlying the campaign and an exposition of how that theory informed the campaign's processes. It is included primarily for the benefit of those with a professional interest in marketing and advertising, but even if you're not a member of that stated target audience, I hope you'll be able to find some application of the theory in your own career.

The history of diffusion theory dates back to work done in Europe in the early 20th century in the fields of anthropology and sociology. French sociologist Gabriel Tarde found that the level of adoption (of a new idea) plotted against time resulted in an S-shaped curve. Approximately forty years later Bryce Ryan and Neal Gross published a study focused on the diffusion and adoption of a new hybrid corn seed among Iowa farmers. The S-shaped diffusion curve made another appearance and it became clear that the diffusion of innovation is indeed a communication process.

Considerable research has been done since that time and multiple models (many of which share a number of common essentials) intended to help explain the diffusion (and adoption) of innovation have been put forward. Everett Rogers proposed that there are four elements in the diffusion of innovations process[28]: (1) the innovation and (2) its communication within (3) a certain social system (4) over a specific period of time. Rogers also addressed the process within the social system itself by establishing five adopter categories and their members' characteristics: (1) innovators, (2) early adopters, (3) early majority, (4) late majority, and (5) laggards.

Additionally, Rogers' diffusion theory model treats the adoption process, the innovation-decision process, rejection and discontinuance, and the consequences of innovation(s). The adoption process is differentiated from the diffusion process in that the latter is a group process occurring within society and the former is pertinent to individual members of the group. Rogers promotes the view that there are five stages of the adoption process: (1) awareness, (2) interest, (3) evaluation, (4) trial, and (5) adoption. Similarly, the closely related innovation-decision process is broken into five stages: (1) acquiring knowledge of an innovation,

(2) forming an attitude toward the innovation, (3) deciding to adopt or reject, (4) implementation of the new idea, and (5) confirmation of the decision. Of course, not all innovations will be accepted—a decision not to adopt an innovation is considered a rejection—and and if that rejection occurs after a trial adoption, whether prompted by dissatisfaction or by a decision for an alternative adoption, it is referred to as discontinuance. Lastly, Rogers' analyzed the consequences, to either a social system or an individual, resulting from the adoption (or rejection) of an innovation with regard the consequences desirability, directness and expectedness.

Diffusion theory has been applied in any number of fields—public health, education, physical sciences, geography, and economics, to name but a few—but of primary concern to the *Would Jesus Discriminate? Campaign* are the social science implications significant to the development of a fully integrated advertising and communication plan which is focused at a predetermined stage of the adoption process. The challenges were principally the following: (1) to create an alternative to the Christian Right's traditionally negative attitudes towards non-heterosexual persons, and (2) to persuade groups of people that the alternative view is indeed viable and should be adopted.

To meet the challenges, the campaign needed to employ communication resources appropriately in order to achieve "breakthrough" at the awareness and interest stages of the adoption process. In that way we could foster the more rapid emergence of the innovators, early adopters and early majority and thus accelerate the rate of diffusion and adoption of attitudes more tolerant toward non-heterosexual persons.

Based on my previous experience in the use of Rogers' model, I established a set of more specific objectives for the *Would Jesus Discriminate? Campaign.* They are as follows:

- Create both a marketing and community engagement strategy appealing to the Millennial generation.[29]
- Create an easy to implement marketing and community engagement program for local churches.
- Generate sufficient resources (both human and financial) to support the short-term creation and medium-term sustenance of cross-country mobilization.
- Secure the financial support of major corporations and faith-based organizations.
- Create participation opportunities for any individuals desirous of creating a more just America.
- Encourage non-heterosexual people to reclaim their faith traditions and "come out" as people of faith
- Encourage congregants of mainstream denominations to exercise voice and vote within their own affiliations.
- Offer people effective tools for addressing discriminatory viewpoints expressed by the Christian Right.
- Spread the campaign's core messages in ten major metropolitan areas in the US to a penetration rate of at least 1% of their respective populations.
- Work toward tipping points[30] at a multiplicity of growth poles.[31]

In conjunction with setting the program goals, the critically important task of selecting and implementing appropriate and effective communication tools for the campaign had to be accomplished. We opted to employ primarily low-cost, low-tech mass media methods that are accessible to/by the majority of the American public; and determined that the campaign was to have significant focus on using newsprint, billboards, bumper stickers, t-shirts, yard signs, and door hangers to generate awareness and interest and to promote dialogue. We also planned for town hall meetings, expected an Internet presence to evolve (both designed commercial websites and non-commercial bulletin board and blog postings) and anticipated noticeable (free) media coverage as our message began to penetrate public consciousness.

In order to assess outcomes, we planned for polling both before and after Phase I in the first campaign location and, as mentioned previously, the results were astonishing: Public Policy Polling reported a 16% increase in positive attitudes towards non-homosexual people at the completion of Phase I in Indianapolis. (A more detailed presentation of the surveys used appears in the next chapter.) Of course it must be pointed out that those surprisingly affirming results, although enormously welcome, are only "early returns" from one location in what is intended to be a much larger campaign—they may or may not be predictive of outcomes in other areas and at other times.

Is it possible to achieve all of stated goals of the *Would Jesus Discriminate? Campaign?* I'll be very satisfied if we accomplish one of them. In fact, I'll be very satisfied if we accomplish any part of one. I am confident that fair-minded people will do the rest. Why? Because each one of us has experienced being "left out" of something, and each of us has a personal story of dealing with the painful feelings aroused by exclusion or rejection. And furthermore, I believe that if each of us were to begin listening carefully to our neighbors' stories of rejection, then our attitudes toward our fellow citizens would begin to shift in a positive way.

I also believe that although neighbors simply listening to each other can be an incredibly powerful tool for initiating change, there are many other ways to foster engaging dialogue. One technique I've used is to invite a neighbor into our home for "movie night" with my family. You might consider viewing "The Power of Harmony" about the members and friends of the Turtle Creek Chorale in Dallas, Texas or "All Aboard," the HBO special about Rosie O'Donnell's cruise with 500 families, all composed of gay/lesbian parents and their children.

If that idea doesn't appeal to you, try a book swap with your neighbor. Or, if you don't like to talk, watch movies or read, just leave a *Would Jesus Discriminate?* coffee mug and a fresh-baked coffee cake on your neighbors' porch. There are a thousand ways to really make a difference, so just customize to suit your own strengths, weaknesses or comfort zone. Design your own campaign—be creative! Or, if you'd prefer, join ours.

In the next few chapters I will describe the people who contributed and the steps we followed in three stages of the Indianapolis campaign and in the initial stage in Minneapolis. Perhaps as you read, you'll be struck with other ways of personalizing the *Would Jesus Discriminate? Campaign* for your individual circumstances and needs.

4

The Campaign in the Beginning

In early 2005, I presented the campaign concept to Matt Foreman, the Executive Director of the National Gay and Lesbian Task Force[32] (NGLTF). At that time his organization and the Human Rights Campaign[33] (HRC) were deeply involved in their own research regarding the best approach to help shift the negative perceptions and attitudes held toward non-heterosexual people by many people of faith. They were trying to determine the optimal language and images to use with members of mainline Protestant denominations, who represent the vast "movable middle" of the American population, and in that process, were not only preparing their own concepts for test markets, but even testing some television ads in major markets.

In spite of the fact that they didn't fund the campaign idea, they did help me make key connections that proved essential to moving forward. Matt Foreman was kind enough to introduce me to Mitchell Gold, who I mentioned earlier in this book and who is the founder of Faith in America. Mitchell and I immediately engaged each other in dialogue and our exchange of ideas continued for a period of about 12 months. By April 2006, we were ready to test a concept that had "morphed" out of the work of FIA and our work at MCC, as well as the HRC and NGLTF programs.

The next step was to choose a local Metropolitan Community Church with vibrant community and strong leadership located in a conservative city with a population of 1 million or more. We were blessed with the choice of Jesus MCC in Indianapolis, Indiana (Marion County). The congregation was willing to take on the potential risks inherent in the campaign. Furthermore, Rev. Jeff Miner, Senior Pastor of Jesus MCC, also serves as the Chairman of the Board of Administration (Directors) for Metropolitan Community Churches worldwide, so he was ideally positioned to assess the denominational impact of the campaign.

Our Indianapolis Campaign began on May 28—the day of the Indianapolis 500 Race, the world's largest single-day sporting event—and ran for approximately 6 weeks. The Campaign featured the following components:

- Four ¾-page newspaper ads, similar to those featured on Faith in America's website, in Sunday editions of The Indianapolis Star (These ads, funded by Mitchell Gold and based on the historical approach of Faith in America, compared current discrimination against non-heterosexual people to past issues involving discrimination such as slavery, voting rights for women and interracial marriage.)
- Twelve billboards asking "Would Jesus Discriminate?" and inviting viewers to a website discussion of that question

- Two thousand yard signs (placed by members of the local congregation) with the same question and website listing
- T-shirts and bumper stickers with the same question and website listing
- Twenty thousand door hangers that posed the central question and invited people to attend a Town Hall Meeting
- A Town Hall Meeting to discuss the religious roots of discrimination and what the Bible really says about homosexuality
- Significant free media coverage that spun off of the foregoing efforts, including local TV news and radio stories and interviews, as well as a national Associated Press story that appeared in major media across the nation, including The Washington Post, The Chicago Tribune, The Miami Herald, The Christian Broadcasting Network, and the Moody Radio Bible Network

To measure impact, Mitchell Gold funded pre- and post-campaign polls conducted by the professional public opinion research company Public Policy Polling out of Raleigh, North Carolina. The two polls comprised identical question lists (so as to provide a reliable before/after comparison) and surveyed 392 and 463 persons on May 24, 2006 and August 24, 2006, respectively. All the participants were self-identifying Christians, 18 years of age or older.[34] As stated earlier, the polling data showed significant positive movement over the three-month period.

The questions asked in the polls can be divided into two key categories: those designed to assess Christians' heartfelt notions about gay people, without reference to religious doctrine, and those designed to test whether respondents were willing to break with traditional church teachings against homosexuality. The former category, dubbed threshold questions because the responses were expected to be closely linked to changing public opinion, were structured to allow respondents to answer affirmatively without contradicting what most Christians have been taught the Bible says about homosexuality. It was intended that answers to the threshold questions would allow assessment of how respondents would, were they not constrained by religious dogma, most likely react to gay people. Questions in the latter category were termed doctrinal questions and it was expected that movement in those responses would occur more slowly and require a more sustained effort.

Below are the key questions, by category, and the percent change noted in responses:

THRESHOLD QUESTIONS

- Should a Christian treat every man and woman as brother and sister?   +12%
- Do you think Jesus loves homosexuals less than he does other people?   + 9%

(9% *fewer* responded "yes")

- Do you believe homosexuals should have all the rights promised to citizens in the US Constitution?   + 5%
- Are you more accepting of homosexuals today than you were six months ago?   +16%

(This last is the really extraordinary number. The pollsters had advised that a 4% to 6% positive shift would be considered a success.)

DOCTRINAL QUESTIONS

- Do you think homosexuals are immoral?   +10%
- Would Jesus be against homosexual marriages?   +13%
- Should Christians oppose laws making it legal for homosexuals to marry?   +4%
- Do you believe the Bible says homosexuality is a sin?   +11%

We organized our analysis of these polling data under five main headings.

- We gained significantly on all the threshold questions—measurable positive progress in response to every question, without exception.
- Movement is not yet detectable on the doctrinal questions. The raw numbers from this question domain were inconsistent with the progress indicated on the threshold questions and seem inexplicable, until one goes deeper into the polling data. A closer look indicated that 11% more of our August respondents reported attending church services more than once a week—a good indicator that the August poll included a significantly higher percentage of members of the Christian Right than had our May poll. Furthermore, cross-tabs in the polling data indicated that a significantly higher portion of these "multiple attendees," 14% to be precise, reported hearing recent sermons against homosexuality from their pastor(s). And, as one would expect, this group was consistently more negative in their responses on the doctrinal questions. When we controlled for the higher percentage of Christian Right members in the August poll, the comparative results on the doctrinal questions indicated stasis. In other words, no ground was lost, but no visible movement had yet taken place on the doctrinal questions. (Incidentally, the fact that we made gains on all the threshold questions despite the presence of significantly more members of the Christian Right in the August survey makes those gains even more impressive.)
- Our Campaign achieved enormous market penetration. In the August poll 51% of respondents remembered seeing our yard signs and billboards. Another 41% remembered seeing our newspaper ads. These are rather extraordinary levels of penetration for a brief six-week campaign and illustrate how

ready people are to engage the religious issues attendant upon homosexuality.

- African Americans opposed gays at a noticeably higher rate than did other identified racial/ethnic groups. African Americans made up 25% of our survey group for the August poll and they reported hearing sermons against homosexuals at a 20% higher rate than other ethnic groups. They also opposed basic civil rights for gay people at an 18% higher rate. (However, 20% of African Americans reported having a more favorable view of gay people than they had had six months ago—one of those threshold questions.)

  The poll also indicated that many fewer African Americans saw the newspaper ads—only 26% as compared to 44% for whites. In contrast, a higher percentage of African Americans noticed the yard signs and billboards—54% compared to 49% for whites.

- Where do we go from here? The post-polling results confirmed our belief that the question "Would Jesus discriminate?" should be the center point of any organized effort to "move the moveable middle" in the US (or anywhere else in the world,) and we agreed that the gains we achieved in Round One of the Indianapolis campaign needed to be reinforced soon if we wished to consolidate those advances and build on our progress. As every advertising expert knows, repetition is the key to creating lasting change in attitudes and beliefs.

Taken together, the movement data on the threshold and doctrinal questions lead us to conclude that the campaign caused Christians across the board to want to be more favorable toward non-heterosexual people, but we had not yet offered them enough information to enable them to break out of the doctrinal "boxes" in which they are so securely entrenched. That conclusion, in turn, triggered some insight into how Jesus MCC, Faith in America and

Metropolitan Community Churches would configure the next round of media work in Indianapolis which launched April 18, 2007.

The data suggested that, in round two, ads needed to begin discussing the Bible at a content level specific enough to reveal the orthodox assertion of biblical condemnation of homosexuality for what is it: an issue of interpretation. (We did not set out to "win" a biblical debate, merely to demonstrate that there are viable alternatives to the traditionally negative biblical interpretations that most people have been taught.)

Furthermore, cost comparisons revealed that we seemed to have achieved more for our money through the use of billboards and yard signs than with other print media. The four newspaper ads cost $42,000 and reached 41% of the metro area population (about 615,000 people.) That works out to be 6.8 cents per person reached, and is certainly cost effective. But the yard signs and billboards ($16,000 to reach 51% (765,000 individuals) of the metro population) cost only 2.1 cents per person reached—a whopping 69% increase in cost-effectiveness over the newspaper ads. (Also, with regard to the view that African Americans are a key group to be reached, yard signs and billboards appeared to have been more valuable than newspaper ads in the Indianapolis area.) Since the key to changing minds is reinforcing a message as many times as possible, and since opting for cost-effectiveness will allow us to greater iterative frequency, we determined that focusing our investment on billboards and yard signs in the next round in Indianapolis would be desirable.

The culminating event of the Indianapolis campaign in 2006 was a community forum. Mitchell Gold, our (MCC's) Moderator Rev. Elder Nancy Wilson, Rev. Jeff Miner and I convened in Indianapolis for a Town Hall Meeting on the topic "Would Jesus Discriminate?" About 400 people[35] attended and, in an atmosphere of sincerity and respect, listened, commented and brought the community conversation, begun with newspaper ads, yard signs and billboards, to a more personal level.

Based on the polling data and the outcomes of the Campaign in 2006, The *WJD? Campaign* Team felt that the appropriate focus of Round Two would be educating Christians about alternative Biblical interpretations regarding homosexuality, and that in Round Three the message ought once again to address the history of religious discrimination. The information planned for Round Two would demonstrate that people can affirm non-heterosexual people while still being true to the scriptures of their faith tradition(s); and the refocusing in Round Three would serve as encouragement not to repeat the mistake(s) of the past.[36]

Jesus MCC, in partnership with Faith in America and Metropolitan Community Churches, initiated Phase II of the campaign on April 18, 2007, with the placement of 22 billboards throughout the city and the launch of the website www.wouldjesusdiscriminate.com. Additionally, 1000 yard signs were put in place, a banner ad on www.google.com directed interested individuals to a survey on our website, and responses were promised for messages left at the toll free number, 1-866-HOPEMCC.

Within its first week, the second phase of the Campaign provoked a response. Several of the church members placing yard signs reported that they were followed by individuals or groups who removed the signs immediately, and within hours of their placement, a number of the signs were defaced or stolen. Additionally, two of the billboards were vandalized with spray paint. (The message on one of the billboards was partially obscured with black paint, and "Lie, lie, lie" was overlaid across the message on the other.[37]) Repair work was undertaken and Rev. Jeff Miner commented to a reporter from the Indianapolis Star, "I think it shows the lengths some people will go to suppress ideas rather than have a dialogue."

Several church leaders in Indianapolis stated publicly that the ad campaign was built on false statements and distorted readings of scripture. Rev. Andy Hunt of Body of Christ Community Church managed to condemn the campaign while still decrying the acts of vandalism, "It ignites passions whenever someone brings a lie against the god you worship, but we can't go down to their level."

In 2007, we decided to broaden the scope of our earlier surveys and really test the validity or "attraction" of the question, Would Jesus discriminate? to any person searching the Internet and, as mentioned earlier, a banner ad ran on www.google.com. The ad simply posed the question "Would Jesus Discriminate?" and invited readers to go to our website, complete a survey, and be entered in contest to attend the US Open and meet Martina Navratilova. Within the first two days of the April billboard postings, fifty people had completed surveys. The survey questions along with those first fifty responses are given below. Please draw your own conclusions.

1 Is the Bible is a reliable guide in every matter regarding what is acceptable behavior?

Yes: 28   No: 20   No opinion: 2

2 In the past, people wrongly used the Bible to deny women equal rights with men.

Agreed: 45   Disagreed: 3   No opinion: 2

3 In the past, people wrongly used the Bible to support slavery and racial segregation.

Agreed: 42   Disagreed: 3   No opinion: 5

4 Today, people wrongly use the Bible to condemn lesbian and gay people.

Agreed: 42   Disagreed: 4   No opinion: 4

5 The Bible contains some stories and teachings that honor and affirm lesbian and gay people and their committed loving

relationships.

Agreed: 37   Disagreed: 5   No opinion: 8

6 Faithful Christians can disagree about what the Bible says about homosexuality.

Agreed: 37   Disagreed: 7   No opinion: 6

7 Some people are born gay.

Agreed: 42   Disagreed: 4   No opinion: 4

8 Lesbian and gay people should have the full rights and protections promised by the US Constitution.

Agreed: 41   Disagreed: 6   No opinion: 3

9 Do you believe that the United States of America government should use the Bible as the basis of constitutional rights and freedoms?

Yes: 18   No: 27   Sometimes: 5

In addition to answering the survey questions, respondents replied to demographic queries:

Are you a US citizen?   Yes: 40   No: 10

(Respondents listed 16 different US states & 2 other countries)

How often do you attend church?

One or more times a week: 28

About once a month: 7

Rarely or never: 15

Do you have a friend or family member who is gay?

Yes: 34   No: 16

What is your sex?   Male: 26   Female: 23

(1 respondent did not identify)

What is your race?   White: 41   Non-white: 9

What is your age group?

Less than 25 years: 18

25 – 40 years: 25

41 – 60 years: 1

Over 60 years: 6

Another aspect of the campaign, which I've not mentioned to this point, was the issuance of press releases to all of the gay media outlets as well as the religious news wires and mainstream media. Rev. Jim Birkitt, our Director of Public Relations and Communications at Metropolitan Community Church, collaborated with Rev.Jeff Miner, Rev. Jimmy Creech and the national press office for Mitchell Gold-Bob Williams to "stoke" the media during the entire campaign. We are indebted to all of them for their faithfulness to this project. Their job was difficult, painful and often thwarted by the anxieties of mainstream media outlets. We are indebted to Clear Channel Communications[38] for its willingness to go the first and second rounds with us in spite of receiving hate mail from the general public as well as threats from some of their clients.

We also conducted a survey on our own website during the campaign—868 individuals from around the world responded. Questions and replies are given below:

	YES	NO	UNSURE
1 Would Jesus discriminate?	137	699	32
2 Does the Bible teach discrimination against people of color?	109	705	43
3 Does the Bible teach discrimination against women?	173	634	46
4 Does the Bible teach discrimination against people with physical and mental challenges?	117	683	46
5 Does the Bible teach discrimination against Jews?	114	690	40
6 Does the Bible teach discrimination against Muslims?	141	645	68
7 Does the Bible teach discrimination against poor people?	90	720	25

	YES	NO	UNSURE
8 Does the Bible teach discrimination against gay and lesbian people?	233	537	72
9 Does the Bible teach that women cannot hold positions of authority over men?	233	438	89
10 Should women serve as clergy or pastors in churches?	496	178	72
11 Did Jesus discriminate against people who were not of his race or ethnicity?	58	651	34
12 Did Jesus discriminate against women in choosing his disciples?	116	539	89
13 Did Jesus discriminate against Jews or any religious identification?	77	613	44
14 Did Jesus discriminate against the gay people of his day?	114	531	97
15 Did Jesus defy the religious authorities of his church/religion as well as the civil authorities of his society to defend the rights of the excluded and oppressed?	452	199	85
16 Did Jesus accept all people into his loving ministry?	606	125	17
17 Are you a US citizen?	546	175	
18 In the US, should our Constitution be amended to allow discrimination against any person or group of persons?	83	499	
19 In the US, should citizens be protected against unreasonable searches of their homes, reading			

REV. DR. CINDI LOVE

	YES	NO	UNSURE
of their e-mails, and wire taps of their phones?	470	170	
20 Would you vote for a constitutional amendment that prohibits the marriage of same-sex couples?	195	387	

Not every participant responded to every question

Of that survey, Rev. Jeff Miner concluded:

> The survey data is consistent with my conviction that, if we really want to change the minds of people who believe it is OK to discriminate against gay people, we must talk about Jesus and His life in a way that is specific enough to help them see that there is an alternative way to interpret what we have been taught that the Bible says about homosexuality.

Other outcomes of the campaign (in both 2006 and 2007) include a significant number of both e-mail responses and telephone messages—some fielded live and others recorded. Earlier e-mails tended more toward the positive, the majority of them thanking us for trying to help gay people, but later e-mails were more varied—roughly half were of the "thank you" variety and the other half a good mix of "f... you" and "you'll burn in hell for lying." The phone calls were generally less positive overall than the e-mails: early callers refused to identify themselves and often wanted to know where we were located. (The assumption was they hoped to find us and shut us up as quickly as possible.) Later callers were more to the point, and more often said we were liars who deserved to burn in hell.

In April of 2007, as Jesus MCC in Indianapolis was launching Phase II of their campaign, All God's Children Metropolitan Community Church in Minneapolis MN initiated their version[39] of the *Would Jesus Discriminate? Campaign.* They began t-shirt distribution on April 17 and unveiled the campaign publicly on April 19 at the Minnesota State Capitol building, where they joined some 5,000 people gathered to support legislation, under consideration at the time, which was friendly to non-traditional families. Yard signs were placed beginning April 22 and public action events were successfully planned and completed. Billboards went up June 11, Rev. Paul Eknes-Tucker was interviewed live on local radio June 14, several other action events were staged in June and July, and All God's Children MCC hosted a July 14 Town Hall meeting. At the time of this writing, the last action event scheduled was t-shirt wearing at the Minnesota State Fair the week of Aug. 19 – 26.

Throughout 2006 – 2007, Faith in America has run campaigns parallel to *Would Jesus Discriminate?* We share a common definition of the problem we want to address: religion-based bigotry. I want to thank Mitchell Gold and Jimmy Creech for permission to cite their campaign overview (see Appendix II) and I want to point out that all of these campaigns have been developed, implemented and tested in diverse markets with minimal investment. When I worked in the corporate world, we used to spend more than $1 million to test just the name of a product. You don't have to spend a fortune to achieve a great result in the marketplace if you have the right theoretical construct, a great tag line and a lot of committed volunteers.

I've shared the theoretical construct with you and I think the tag line *Would Jesus Discriminate?* clearly worked for us. Now, let me explain why it is so important for individuals and organizations who share common causes around the issues of discrimination against non-heterosexual people to collaborate in these campaigns.

We can mobilize the largest volunteer base in America, starting with the absolute largest units of that base, churches. There are more than 2 billion identified members of churches in America today and their charitable contributions make up the primary funding for their respective organizations. When appropriate groundwork and robust communications are established, churches can work very effectively with secular human rights and social action organizations. I cherish the relationships that Metropolitan Community Church shares with its strategic alliance partners, the HRC, the NGLTF, the Religious Roundtable, the Institute for Welcoming Resources and others.

I am not a professional researcher or forecaster, but my "armchair analysis" says that, although we are clearly divided on issues of scriptural authority, human rights for gays, and how/if such issues should be addressed legislatively, the simple majority seems to be moving toward the idea that non-heterosexuals deserve the same rights as all other human beings. Since I have two gay children, and one of them is married to her partner, I have high hopes that my grandchildren will live in a much more tolerant world than we do at this moment.

5

Solidarity will Move us Forward

The gay and lesbian community's maturing political awareness has produced progressive secular organizations like HRC and NGLTF that focus on issues such as hate crimes legislation, marriage equality, workplace non-discrimination, and adoption rights— concerns related to protecting non-heterosexual people from violence as well as promoting their rights to "regular" domestic lives. They have also created departments or divisions within their own organizations to work with faith-based entities and communities of faith in order to "change the conversation"[40] and "reclaim from the right wing the true meaning of moral values."[41]

I support that work 100 percent and I stand in solidarity with the brilliant and dedicated activists of those organizations as we pressure our political leaders to "wake up." Furthermore, I am honored to serve also with a number of equally devoted and thoughtful faith leaders in addressing some of the same issues from a non-secular perspective.

I recently traveled to Washington DC with the Clergy Call to Justice and Equality hosted by the Human Rights Campaign (HRC). I joined 220 religious leaders from around the country and from diverse faith traditions to speak of our support for the Matthew Shepard Act and the employment non-discrimination act (ENDA). We told our stories on behalf of ourselves, our communities, our denominations, and our churches, mosques and synagogues. We told our stories in Congressional and Senate offices, in the press, and in candid conversations with each other.

The President of HRC, Joe Solmonese said,

> All day long as HRC staffers escorted [the faith leaders] around Hill offices there was a crackle of excitement in the air. That energy sparked unexpectedly in the morning as staff worked to arrange the more than 220 leaders on risers for the photo op and press event when they suddenly, completely unprompted by HRC staff or anyone else, started singing "We Shall Overcome" and "This Little Light of Mine." The gentle power of their voices spoke volumes about the ground we were breaking.[42]

It was an amazing day. I was blessed in being able to tell how the TORO Company had non-discrimination policies in place when I worked there; and I was saddened to report that the same thing was not true where my brother had been employed—he was discharged from his job with a state agency when he identified himself as a person living with HIV. As an individual, it was important for me to speak the truths of my own life and, as a cleric, it was critical for me to bear witness to the experiences of our congregants in their workplaces.

My denomination, Metropolitan Community Church, has been a prominent advocate for change in society's treatment of non-heterosexual individuals since 1969 when Troy Perry conducted the first Holy Union and then filed a lawsuit for its ratification in New York. We are honored now by our ability to join hands with progressive organizations, both secular and spiritual, around a much larger issue: the use of religious-based bigotry to oppress people—all people, including non-heterosexual people.

I believe that those who are convicted of the worth and dignity of all human beings need to call upon mainstream churches not simply to recognize their biases, but fully to **repent of their bigotry**. I also believe that the only way to present that message is to engage people in deliberate study of Scripture while using language they already know.

In general, people repent only if they become convicted that they are wrong or have sinned. As a Southerner, brought up to follow the *seven steps of salvation*, and well-versed in the emotional appeals of an "altar call," I understand that perspective all too well. It took the crucible of my life experience to convince me to dig deeper into my own understanding of Scripture.

Most clergy of mainline churches confine their consideration of gay issues (and some do so without even being conscious of the limitation) to discussions of same-sex marriage, adoption and ordination. They stay away from the essential questions like "Would Jesus discriminate? In fact, part of the Anglican Communion seems to have side-stepped its own campaign, *"What Would Jesus Do?"* for an all-out war on homosexuals. This is incongruent and it is harmful.

However, it does make sense—well; it's at least understandable—when you take modern religious history into account. Traditionally, churches have viewed homosexuality as a sin and non-heterosexual people as "non-Christians." Therefore, when homosexuals want to marry, adopt children and serve as clergy—you know, do all the things that Christians have historically done—it creates havoc in the rank and file. These churches don't want to throw away centuries of practice and theological insight, and surely they don't want to admit to being wrong. (The prospect of losing the financial support of their congregants is likely a pretty powerful disincentive, as well.) Yet, we are called to reform ourselves.

Indeed, Church history is actually filled with instances of transformation. Jesus Himself called people to rethink faith and Scripture, hope and love. Martin Luther's theses were faith-shaking for his contemporaries but spurred the Church's movement along the path of necessary change and growth. The Christian faith is not and cannot be static—God doesn't change, but times do and humans do—and Christians must be about the business of moving whatever has gotten in the way of being Jesus-like and working out how to live as God created us to be. "The tradition," Rob Bell says, "...is painting, not making copies of the same painting over and over."[43] We must be continually "born again" in our faith—one that is alive only when it is tearing down walls and building up hope.[44]

Let's look at what is happening to denominations and churches right now. A great portion of the information that follows is taken from a brilliant study of denominational responses to non-heterosexuals' issues done by the National Gay & Lesbian Task Force.[45] I want to thank Matt Foreman and the other leaders of The Task Force for the development and dissemination of this critical research and for allowing me to share parts of that work with you.

Spiritual organizations and religious leaders who are supportive of non-heterosexual issues face multiple discriminations and because of the groundbreaking nature of their work, many of these organizations endure extreme opposition and struggle just to survive. Some of the organizations have been working for gay equality since (and a few even before) the inception of the modern gay rights movement. Most of them are under-funded, under-staffed and often under-appreciated.

The report goes on to say that these organizations and congregations have shouldered most of the responsibility of educating religious people about the non-heterosexual community, and that they provide support for thousands within that community. They bind up the wounds created by damaging right-wing religion and their work allows non-heterosexual people to find spiritual homes in churches and congregations across the spectrum of American faith traditions. They have often been the unsung spiritual strength of the non-heterosexual community.

Non-heterosexual people of faith and their religious allies have unique skills and resources for combating the members of the Christian Right. They have the potential to be the primary force in reframing issues of faith and values in Christian discourse in favor of a more just and progressive agenda. Their opposition is, however, immense, well-organized, and largely unanswered by the progressive community.

Indeed, groups operating from within various denominations that apply for funds and support from forward-thinking foundations and secular societies are frequently met with the response, "We don't fund religious groups" or "We don't fund religious groups unless they're ecumenical." Secular progressives' continued discomfort with assisting religious progressives has allowed the conservative movement to establish a major foothold in America's churches, and if this trend is not reversed, the forces of intolerance will produce significant economic and social losses.

The Institute for Religion and Democracy and other anti-gay

organizations profiled in the NGLTF report represent a massive "shadow conservative movement" pumping millions of dollars into anti-gay movements in America's religious institutions. Their activists, many of whom are connected at the highest levels of the conservative movement, are working behind the scenes to influence the opinions of tens of millions of otherwise moderate Americans, using fear, homophobia, and calls for religious purity in organizations that hold great personal and spiritual significance for their members.

Just in case you think the report or I am overstating the case, let me share two e-mails with you. These came to me in the first few days of the 2006 *Would Jesus Discriminate? Campaign* in Indianapolis; names and addresses that would overtly identify the senders have been altered, but the body of the messages, language and syntax, are quoted exactly as received.

> From: XXX [mailto:YYY@hotmail.com]
> Sent: Tue 7/25/2006 5:15 PM
> To: Rev. Dr. Cindi Love
> Subject: Would Jesus Discriminate?
>
> Yes he would... He Did! He didn't just ask the people to leave the temples he went in and overturned the tables and threw them out! That is what we should do with sinners. Not races, not people, but people who commit sin in our homes and lands. Homosexuality is a sin! To discriminate means to treat recognize a difference. You bet he did and not only did he discriminate but he handled it head on. Stop trying to sugar coat the truth because you are afraid to stand up for what is right. People do wrong things. We need to act and follow Christ example of attacking the sin and not the sinner. He didn't beat anyone up but he threw them right out.

We need to ban the practice and throw out anyone not willing to abide by Gods laws of happiness.

Have a nice day,

And then,

From: XXX [mailto:YYY@hoboline.net]
Sent: Tue 7/25/2006 7:18 PM
To: Rev. Dr. Cindi Love
Subject: Would Jesus Discriminate?

I like your message, but God will be very discriminate against sin. We are not to discriminate against a soul just sin. Come on tell the truth.

Let's admit, at a gut level, when we hear the question "Would Jesus discriminate? it seems like the answer must be, "No!" But, as you can see, the individuals who wrote me believe that He did and does. They believe that I am, *by virtue of my sexual orientation alone,* a sinner.

We live in a time when many churches are leading the effort to influence legislation specifically designed to exclude gay and transgender people from equal protection under the law. In the United States, attempts are being made to amend both federal and state constitutions to ensure that non-heterosexual couples never gain access to the same legal rights as their heterosexual counterparts. The practical effect of these proposed amendments will be to deprive non-heterosexual couples of basic human rights, such as being present at a loved one's bedside in times of grief and/ or illness or being accorded the legal standing of a spouse, or even family, in times of bereavement.

Since so many churches are invoking the name of Jesus to justify this assault, I invite thoughtful people everywhere to ask again the famous question of the Anglican community…

What would Jesus do?

The answer is not hard to find, according to Rev. Jeff Miner. The following is excerpted from Jesus MCC's website:

> One of the central themes of Jesus' life was a recurring conflict with the Pharisees, a powerful group of legalistic religious leaders. The Pharisees were waiting for the Messiah to come, and they believed that would happen only when their entire nation became righteous. So, in their minds, anyone who failed to follow their detailed rules was bringing down a curse on their nation and worthy of contempt.

Sound familiar?

The list of people despised by the Pharisees was long:

- *The Samaritans were considered religious heretics and ethnically impure.*
- *Sick people were believed to be sinners whom God was punishing.*
- *Women were deemed unworthy of discipleship.*
- *Tax collectors and Roman soldiers were regarded as the enemy.*
- *The poor, who had neither the time nor resources to maintain rigorous rites of religious purity, were thought to be beyond God's grace.*

> *Jesus emphatically rejected each of these prejudices, [as you can read for yourself in] John 4:1 – 42; Luke 10:29 – 37; John 9:1 – 34; Luke 8:1 – 3; Matt 11:16 – 19; Matt 5:38 – 48; and Matt 9:18 – 26… The Gospels are clear. Jesus refused to be bound by cultural prejudice. Repeatedly, he defended the oppressed against narrow-minded religious and political leaders.*[46]

REV. DR. CINDI LOVE

The Gospels also tell me that we have to stand in solidarity with those who share our commitment to ending religiously-based bigotry and the discrimination it engenders. The apostles would today be forgotten men, forgotten names from a forgotten century, had they not stayed in Jerusalem as Jesus told them to do before that pivotal Pentecost. And in the present day, our non-heterosexual neighbors need us to stick around and speak up like Peter and his associates did (speaking diverse languages, I might add!) so many long years ago.

6

Speaking Up

Shortly after the launch of the 2006 campaign in Indianapolis I was back at the MCC offices in Los Angeles and crossed the street to eat lunch. As I stood waiting to order I noticed a couple (obviously a gay man and his mother) in line with me. I asked the woman if she was visiting, she said, "Yes!" I asked her son what they planned to do and we continued to visit.

When the woman shared that she was from Indianapolis, I said, "Wow, we have a new campaign going on there! I'm the Executive Director of Metropolitan Community Churches." She paused for just a second, then exclaimed, "Oh, my... the 'Would Jesus Discriminate?' deal!" I replied affirmatively and then she said, "When I saw the first sign, I thought 'Are they crazy? People will want to kill them.' Then I said to myself, 'NO! Someone has to ask that question.' Now I just feel scared."

I asked her, "Does West Hollywood feel safe? She said, "Yes, everyone here is nice to us and they take care of my son." I said, "You know, that's a conscious decision by citizens who probably hadn't even thought to consider the question until someone else asked 'Could there be a place for gay and lesbian people that is welcoming, even incorporated around their interests?'"

She replied, "You know, that's right. You are crazy, you know, but I'm glad you are." Somehow, I didn't mind being called crazy that afternoon.

Studies show that people typically are not able to hear truth that is inconsistent with their core beliefs until those core beliefs are directly addressed and reshaped. We saw dozens of letters resulting from our Indianapolis Campaign that said essentially, "My negative beliefs about gay and transgender people can't be discriminatory because my beliefs are based on the Bible and the Bible is God's revealed truth."

In our effort to undermine the religious roots of discrimination against non-heterosexual people, we must tackle that mindset directly. We have to confront it in the media and in our local gathering places—the stores where we shop, the schools that our children attend and the churches where we worship. And we know that change is possible. Let me tell you Brent Childers' story.[47]

Childers, a conservative Christian living in North Carolina, was sitting at the dinner table and had just declared, "You don't want queers taking over society!" when he was startled by his 62-year-old mother asking the question, "Is that a very Christ-like attitude to have?" Because of that unexpected query from an unexpected spokeswoman, Brent was forced to reflect upon his uncharitable outlook, his self-righteous attitude and his acid tone. His mom's words, he says, were like "an alarm going off. It was like, 'Hold on. Let's think about this a bit.'"

Some months later, Childers remarked to another conservative Christian, "I don't think a homosexual can practice that lifestyle and be a Christian." The woman immediately disagreed and told him about a friend who was both gay and devoutly Christian.

Nudged for the second time, Childers began to consider seriously how he could reconcile his position that homosexuals are "wicked, unclean people with no chance of eternal life" with the loving underpinnings of his Christian faith. His questions propelled him along a spiritual journey that took him away from prejudice.

That journey presented him with an unlikely opportunity when Childers' advertising agency was approached about creating a series of ads designed to prod anti-gay religious folks into thinking about how religion was used to justify such wrongs as slavery and denying women the right to vote. (Faith in America was the prospective client.)

After praying, Childers agreed to help create the ads. He drew upon his own 180° perspective shift as he developed the layouts, and the resulting nine ads were emotionally gripping and intellectually compelling.

One of the ads pictured US Supreme Court Justice Clarence Thomas, who is African-American, with his wife, Virginia, who is white, and posed the question, "Offense before God?" The ad included additional text explaining that the Bible was cited as recently as 1967 in defense of laws banning interracial marriage; it appeared in *Roll Call*, a newspaper targeted at members of Congress, during the confirmation hearings for Justice Samuel Alito.

Another ad showed white-robed Klansmen in front of burning crosses. The text read: "Remember when the cross was used to promote discrimination towards people of color? Let's not use it today to promote that same attitude towards people who are gay." At the bottom of each ad was the appeal: "Religion-based bigotry.

Let's end it now and forever."

Faith in America's executive director, Jimmy Creech, wanted the ads to spark a national conversation about how the Bible is still being used to hurt people. Creech, who is heterosexual, felt the sting of anti-gay bigotry cloaked in religion when he was defrocked as a Methodist minister in 1999 for officiating at a gay couple's Holy Union. He and Brent Childers know that prejudices thrive only when unexamined. For Christians who have not yet embraced gay friends and neighbors, a simple question can be wonderfully life-changing: "Is that a very Christ-like attitude to have?"[48]

Since the completion in Indianapolis of Phase I of the *Would Jesus Discriminate? Campaign* in July 2006, articles and books have been flooding the stands, and faith leaders in many traditions are speaking out publicly. I don't know if there is any causal relationship, but I believe in great marketing and the movement of the Holy Spirit. The work of Faith in America, Jesus MCC and Metropolitan Community Churches has been blessed by a lot of publicity, and several other bright lights of promise have also emerged in the public sphere. Please allow me to share them with you.

In early September of 2006, a number of Christian leaders whose organizations touch the lives of about 32% of the American population, met in Dallas, Texas, for the Bishops and Elders Council. At that time they agreed upon a joint statement calling for an end to the homophobia and heterosexism in churches, as well as a reaffirmation of Jesus' message of love, welcome and acceptance of all people. Their statement is reproduced below:

STATEMENT BY BISHOPS AND ELDERS COUNCIL
On September 11, 2001, some leading Christian extremists portrayed the tragedy of 9/11 as God's judgment on America for the presence of gays and lesbians. The intervening years have witnessed an alarming escalation of religion-based, anti-gay

attacks by both political leaders and religious groups.

Today, on the fifth anniversary of the 9/11 attacks, we, as leaders representing organizations that touch the lives of 98 million Americans, are united in our rejection of all forms of fear-based religion, all political manipulation in the name of Jesus, and governmental hostility toward gays, lesbians, bisexuals and transgender persons, especially that hostility that uses Christianity as an excuse to divide society and demonize minorities.

Today, as Christian leaders who have gathered in Council in Dallas, Texas, we proclaim that discrimination, rejection, scapegoating, and oppression of gay people and their families are incompatible with the Christian ethic of love – and are not spiritual, democratic, patriotic, or fair.

Today, we announce that the anti-gay agenda against gay, lesbian, bisexual and transgender is effectively over. Thanks to a rapidly growing movement of churches and faith leaders in communities across the United States, thousands of churches now embrace Jesus' message that "whosoever will may come," and open their doors in welcome to same-gender-loving people of faith. Gay, lesbian, bisexual and transgender Christians, along with their families and allies, now have the option of nurturing their spiritual lives in faith communities that celebrate and welcome all of God's creation.

Motivated by our Christian faith and to further our nation's founding goals of justice and equality for all, we call upon all people of goodwill to work actively for an end to discrimination against gay, lesbian, bisexual, and transgender persons by:

- **Realizing** that the relationships of same-gender loving couples are equal in every way to heterosexual couples and are worthy of both the right to civil marriage and the rites of Christian marriage;
- **Reaffirming** the rights of gays, lesbians, bisexuals, and

transgender persons to full equality under the law, including adoption rights, employment and housing protections, and the right to openly serve in the US military;

- **Refusing** to cooperate with or support political or religious leaders who caricature and condemn the lives of gays and lesbians;
- **Refuting** the ex-gay notion that sexual orientation and gender identity can and should be changed.

As unified followers of Christ, reclaiming our faith, we commit to speak boldly with our own communities and the larger culture from out of our experience as those who have been both oppressed and oppressor. We will communicate God's incessant call for justice, wholeness and peace and work to equip ourselves and others to take concrete action to achieve God's loving shalom.

The Bishops and Elders Council further commits to continued work on behalf of all people oppressed or marginalized by poverty, immigration policies, HIV/AIDS, addictions, classism, sexism, ageism, or violence.[49]

In addition to that statement out of Dallas, let me tell you about Jack Rogers' history-making text. In *Jesus, the Bible and Homosexuality* Rogers says,

> The church is being torn apart by controversy over whether people who are homosexual can have full rights of membership.... How we choose to respond to this issue is a test of who we will become as a nation.... We in the church are not living according to the ideals of our Savior and Sovereign, Jesus Christ, when we discriminate unjustly against any group of people in our midst. To act unjustly weakens our witness to Christ in the world."

He goes on to cite a report from a Presbyterian committee on

REV. DR. CINDI LOVE

pluralism which determined that the church must address the issue of how the scriptures are to be interpreted, or risk the continuing obstruction of its ministry/mission and a potential spiral into damaging division. He continues:

> The debate over homosexuality crosses all religious lines and is of critical interest in American culture. It is not going away and all of us need to be as informed as possible to cope constructively with what affects all of us…. Some fear that any change in attitude will mean the end of Western civilization as we know it.

Rogers quotes James Dobson of Focus on the Family at that point, and then concludes with the following:

> I have had a change of mind and heart. I had never really studied the issue of the status in the church of people who are homosexual. I opposed homosexuality reflexively— it was what I thought Christians were supposed to do. However, studying this issue in depth for the first time brought me to a new understanding of the biblical texts and of God's will for our church. The process was both very serious and painful. I wasn't swayed by the culture or pressured by academic colleagues. I changed my mind initially by going back to the Bible and taking seriously its central message for our lives.
>
> Since then, my new conviction has been reinforced from many sources. I have studied how the church changed its mind on other moral issues. I worked through how the church, guided by the Holy Spirit in understanding the Scriptures, reversed our prohibitions against ordination to leadership for African Americans, women and divorced and remarried people.[50]

Let me echo Jack's words: I, too, have experienced a profound change of mind and heart as a result of serious, often painful, study and prayer. If you feel sure that homosexual Christians should not have equal rights in the Church (or if you are convinced that Christianity and homosexuality are mutually exclusive) I urge you to walk though *Jesus, the Bible and Homosexuality* as well as Rev. Jeff Miner and John Tyler Connoley's book *The Children are Free.*[51] Give yourself permission to consider the essential questions that you thought you already knew the answers to. Jesus said to his disciples, "If you hold to my teaching, you are really my disciples. Then you will know the truth, and the truth will set you free."[52]

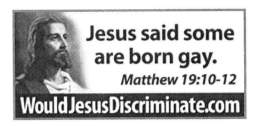

REV. DR. CINDI LOVE

7

Let's Do Better

Throughout history, the Bible's words, and human interpretations thereof, have been used to support injurious institutions and validate blatant bigotry. Within the past 200 years alone, passages from the Bible have been used to justify slavery, to oppress women and to exclude homosexuals from the sacraments. Not until 2006 did the Episcopalian House of Bishops consider a resolution apologizing for its complicity in the institution of slavery[53] and the Southern Baptist Convention's 1991 Resolution on Human Sexuality states "Scripture condemns any abuse of sexuality... and homosexuality."[54] Many of us have attended churches or lived in places where women are noticeable absent from positions of leadership.

Many of us can remember the day we first saw a person of color enter our churches. I remember how white Christians got up from their seats and moved to the other side of the aisle, and I remember the looks on their faces as they did so. I saw a similar division in Shreveport, Louisiana in 1976 when my then-husband and I welcomed a new song director who was black. Our church eventually split, not yet ready to deal with the issues of race and class.

Can we glean anything from these experiences or will we continue to downplay the significance of the Church having condoned, or even promoted, discriminatory practices? Will we ignore the agenda of the Christian Right in the United States? That agenda achieves its aims only as long as churches continue to promote the idea that it is an abominable sin to be non-heterosexual and furthermore that it is a choice to be so.

Many people are quick to argue that being black or female is quite different from "the willful sin of homosexuality." Experiences of marginalization are so uniquely internalized and institutionalized that this point becomes and issue which separates people from one another and from the solidarity we can find in crossing the lines of our own oppression in order to build communities of faith. Jesus didn't say anything at all about homosexuals, much less their "choices." Yes, that's right; Jesus, the central figure in the Christian Scripture, the one His followers seek to emulate, said nothing at all about homosexuality—perhaps He didn't think it was all that important. Jesus chose to include ALL people. Jesus created common bonds and community regardless of gender, social status, ethnicity, cultural background, and religious tradition.

But conservatives who exclude homosexuals from full citizenship in the Beloved Community have plenty of opinions. They say that the Bible records God's judgment against the sin of homosexuality from its first mention in scripture; that homosexuals are somehow inferior in moral character; and that homosexuals are willfully sinful, sexually promiscuous and threatening and deserve punishment for their own acts. The Church is repeating the mistakes of the past: once again claiming Divine Word to support their human dogma. We are thankful that most Christians no longer believe in racial or gender hierarchy; and we firmly believe, as Jack Rogers says so gracefully and succinctly, that a Christological approach, which uses the whole Bible with Jesus as its central character, can enable the church to change its mind and heart on issues of homosexuality.[55]

Rodney Stark, a sociologist at Baylor University and one of my favorite resources, also takes a Christ-centered approach to the issues of human interaction. He says:

> Jesus asserted a revolutionary concept of moral equality, not only in words, but in deeds. Over and over he ignored status boundaries and worked with stigmatized people, including Samaritans, publicans, immoral women and various other outcasts, giving divine sanction to an inclusive society. It was in precisely that spirit that Paul admonished: "there is neither Jew nor Greek, there is neither bond nor free, there is neither male nor female, for ye are all one in Christ Jesus." Regardless of worldly inequalities, the revolutionary new doctrine of Christianity asserted there is real social equality in the most important sense; in the eyes of God and in the life to come. Paul warned slave masters of this "He who is both their master and yours is in heaven and there is no partiality with Him." The writers of the New Testament made it crystal clear that equality in the eyes of God has implications for how people ought to be treated in this world.[56]

The (scriptural) debate about homosexuality focuses on, at most, eight texts: Genesis 19:1 – 29; Judges 19:1 – 30; Leviticus 18: 1 – 30; Leviticus 20:1 – 27; Romans 1:21 – 28; 1 Corinthians 6:9 – 17; 1 Timothy 1:3 – 13; and Jude 7. Four of the passages date from pre-Christian times and a fifth text (Jude) refers to Old Testament events. None of the texts is about Jesus, and not a single one of them includes any of His words.

Rowan Williams, the Archbishop of Canterbury, has said that conservative Christians who cite the Bible to condemn homosexuality are misreading a key passage in Romans,[57] and there are a great number of well-researched, scholarly works that examine and discuss the aforementioned passages. Rather than investing in more books, though, you may prefer to peruse online resources. Both www.jesusmcc.org and www. wouldjesusdiscriminate.com have information (and links to information) related to the interpretation and understanding of the few biblical passages that touch on same-sex relations.

In addition to excellent analyses of the supposedly "anti-gay" passages, the websites also present Christ-centered, insightful, non-heterosexual-affirming commentaries on several other biblical texts. Since those discussions are so readily available, I'll not quote them at length here. I do, however, encourage you to explore the writings and sermons of Rev. Jeff Miner[58] in particular. His work is well-prepared, deeply thoughtful and motivated by his desire "to rescue the Bible from misinterpretations driven by cultural prejudice, so its true message of grace, hope, and peace can come through."[59] Furthermore, although the content is scholarly, Rev. Jeff's presentations are quite accessible and could serve as starting points for dialogue with your family, co-workers or clergy.

The debate about interpretations of scripture regarding homosexuality can continue for another 200 years if we are willing for it to be so. If we don't want to repeat the sort of harm caused by our history of discrimination against women and

REV. DR. CINDI LOVE

people of color, we can make a course correction now. Oliver "Buzz" Thomas, a Baptist minister, wrote an Op-Ed piece on the credibility of religion for *USAToday* in November of 2006, which addressed not only contextual understanding of scripture but also scientific understanding of homosexuality. Parts of that article are excerpted here:

> What if Christian leaders are wrong about homosexuality? I suppose, much as a newspaper maintains its credibility by setting the record straight, church leaders would need to do the same:
>
> Correction: Despite what you might have read, heard or been taught throughout your churchgoing life, homosexuality is, in fact, determined at birth and is not to be condemned by God's followers.
>
> Religion's only real commodity, after all, is its moral authority. Lose that, and we lose our credibility. Lose credibility, and we might as well close up shop.
>
> It's happened to Christianity before, most famously when we dug in our heels over Galileo's challenge to the biblical view that the Earth, rather than the sun, was at the center of our solar system. You know the story. Galileo was persecuted for what turned out to be incontrovertibly true. For many, especially in the scientific community, Christianity never recovered.
>
> This time, Christianity is in danger of squandering its moral authority by continuing its pattern of discrimination against gays and lesbians in the face of mounting scientific evidence that sexual orientation has little or nothing to do with choice. To the contrary, whether sexual orientation arises as a result of the

mother's hormones or the child's brain structure or DNA, it is almost certainly an accident of birth. The point is this: Without choice, there can be no moral culpability.

As a former "the Bible says it, I believe it, that settles it" kind of guy, I am sympathetic with any Christian who accepts the Bible at face value. But here's the catch. Leviticus is filled with laws imposing the death penalty for everything from eating catfish to sassing your parents. If you accept one as the absolute, unequivocal word of God, you must accept them all.

The truth is that mainstream religion has moved beyond animal sacrifice, slavery and the host of primitive rituals described in Leviticus centuries ago. Selectively hanging onto these ancient proscriptions for gays and lesbians exclusively is unfair according to anybody's standard of ethics. We lawyers call it "selective enforcement," and in civil affairs it's illegal.

A better reading of Scripture starts with the book of Genesis and the grand pronouncement about the world God created and all those who dwelled in it. "And, the Lord saw that it was good." If God created us and if everything he created is good, how can a gay person be guilty of being anything more than what God created him or her to be?

Turning to the New Testament, the writings of the Apostle Paul at first lend credence to the notion that homosexuality is a sin, until you consider that Paul most likely is referring to the Roman practice of pederasty, a form of pedophilia common in the ancient world. Successful older men often took boys into their homes as concubines, lovers or sexual slaves. Today, such sexual exploitation of minors is no longer tolerated. The point is that the sort of long-term, committed, same-sex relationships that are being debated today are not addressed in the New Testament. It distorts the biblical witness to apply verses written in one historical context (i.e. sexual exploitation of children) to contemporary situations between two monogamous partners of the same sex. Sexual promiscuity is condemned by the Bible whether it's between gays or straights. Sexual fidelity is not.

For those who have lingering doubts, dust off your Bibles and take a few hours to reacquaint yourself with the teachings of Jesus. You won't find a single reference to homosexuality. There are teachings on money, lust, revenge, divorce, fasting and a thousand other subjects, but there is nothing on homosexuality. Strange, don't you think, if being gay were such a moral threat?

On the other hand, Jesus spent a lot of time talking about how we should treat others. First, he made clear it is not our role to judge. It is God's. ("Judge not lest you be judged." Matthew 7:1) And, second, he commanded us to love other people as we love ourselves.

So, I ask you. Would you want to be discriminated against? Would you want to lose your job, housing or benefits because of something over which you had no control? Better yet, would you like it if society told you that you couldn't visit your lifelong partner in the hospital or file a claim on his behalf if he were murdered?

The suffering that gay and lesbian people have endured at the hands of religion is incalculable, but they can look expectantly to the future for vindication. Scientific facts, after all, are a stubborn thing. Even our religious beliefs must finally yield to them as the church in its battle with Galileo ultimately realized.[60]

Recently, I was exposed to a slightly different approach to the issue of inclusion when I read "Interpretation of the Christian Message," a paper by Melanie Martinez, a seminarian at Perkins School of Theology in Dallas TX. The paper, which explores the movement of the Holy Spirit within the people who are the church, and draws on the work of José Comblin,[61] points out the degree to which the Holy Spirit acts "as a partner within the triune God, rather than [as] an afterthought."[62] Martinez asserts (with documented support from Comblin) that the church, which is the sum total of its members' diversity, is called to bring about the realm of God; that is, to increase freedom, life and community by freeing itself from an alienating past. Additionally, she says that the Holy Spirit engenders unity through diversity by creating within Christians a powerful inclination to move toward others in friendship and love; and furthermore, that it is that very difference-spanning unity which will ultimately allow the full realization of the kingdom of God.

The *Would Jesus Discriminate? Campaign* insists that non-heterosexual people are no "afterthought" of God and confronts the insidious harms of prejudice and discrimination. It asserts that the message of the Gospel is the lens through which the whole of scripture is to be interpreted. Love and compassion, justice and peace are at the very core of the life and ministry of Jesus, and inclusion is a key component of the Christ's essential message. If we interpret the Bible literally, we must still support slavery, the subjugation of women and the belief that the world as we know it was created in seven 24-hour days. We will also have to condone polygamy but punish man/man sex (and some assorted dietary transgressions) with death, while tolerating woman/woman sex. But those are patently absurd outcomes, and we don't interpret the Bible in that way. Jesus said that all the law and the prophets—all the moral and ethical teaching the Bible—can be summed up in loving God and loving our neighbors as ourselves. It is not an act of love toward our non-heterosexual neighbors to discriminate against them.

> I have a hope and faith, that one day when all persons recognize their sexual orientation they will do it with high self esteem... and be totally accepted by their family, friends, religious community and government. And that the words gay, straight, lesbian, bisexual, transgender, etc. will have no meaning... or place in our conversation.
>
> *Mitchell Gold, Founder and President*
> *Faith In America, Inc.*

8

One Year Later

In marketing, what really counts is whether the cash register rings. For us, in the case of this campaign, the total sales equivalent is the number of people who actually noticed a yard sign, billboard, t-shirt, door hanger or newspaper ad and then shared with their neighbors what they thought about the question.

On June 1, 2006, the website www.ChurchMarketingSucks. com (a special interest site for church marketers) posted its review of the first phase of the campaign in Indianapolis. The text of the initial posting is reproduced below along with a representative sample of responses. All told there were 25 comments made, 23 of which were posted two months of the original review and, as is typically the case with linked responses, the topic(s) of the conversation(s) tended to be multi-focal. As you will see, the opinions ran from "this campaign is horrible" to "this campaign is great," and more than one or two individuals could barely comment on the marketing aspect because they had so much to say about the subject matter of the campaign.

June 1, 2006

Would Jesus Discriminate?

2,000 yard signs, four newspaper ads, 650 bumper stickers, 720 T-shirts and 25,000 door hangers have appeared in the Indianapolis area, all promoting Jesus Metropolitan Community Church as a part of a $55,000 ad campaign. And the campaign focuses on homosexuality.

"Do you know someone who is homosexual? Would you give your life for that person? Jesus did," the church's ad says....

[Pastor Jeff] Miner said a future ad in a Sunday edition of The Star will show a group of Klansmen around a burning cross with a headline, "Remember a time when a symbol of love was used as a symbol of hate?"

In addition to the campaign, the church is also holding a town hall meeting on homosexuality and the Bible.

However you feel about their position, their campaign and approach is an interesting example.

Posted by Kevin D. Hendricks at June 1, 2006 10:18 AM

Comments

Love the sinner, hate the sin would definitely be the classic line..... Oddly enough I don't see anything about

REV. DR. CINDI LOVE

the second 1/2 of the phrase anywhere on their site.......
Posted by: Peter at June 1, 2006 2:06 PM

They are right, Jesus didn't discriminate. However...

I poked around their site, and there are some serious problems. They are rewriting Matthew 8:5-13 to say that the Centurion and his servant were gay lovers. They also rewrite the Bible verses about homosexuality and the sin of Sodom that it was not about homosexuality at all.

There is even an audio article using the teaser of "What does the Bible say about Transgenderism?" using the story of Jesus bringing the little girl back to life. Granted I haven't listened to the audio, but unless that is just an attention-getting headline...

Their point is true – don't treat them with anything less that Jesus' love. However, I wouldn't recommend attending a church that perverts God word to match their lifestyle - : (
Posted by: Matt L at June 2, 2006 7:52 AM

On a tactical level, it's great marketing, in that the tagline is simple, it's easy to remember/talk about, and it makes the reader think and therefore hopefully forms an opinion.

It's horrible marketing at a strategic level, though. The anti-homosexuality (for want of a better term) crowd dominates opinions in the media, the government, and across most all churches.

From that standpoint, the campaign is wasted money and therefore bad marketing.

Posted by: Roland at June 2, 2006 1:24 PM

This site was so disturbing to me theologically I just could not get past it to even think about the merits of the campaign itself. Frankly, Jesus does "discriminate"…

… I'm concerned these folks are attempting to speak for the God I serve.

I realize that my beliefs on individual issues like this are not the focus of this website, but I just want to go on record is being really bothered by this open perversion of God's Word.

Posted by: Gene Mason at June 2, 2006 3:04 PM

Have checked out the marketing campaign and find it to be very interesting and love based. It offers so many people an option to find God without being condemned because they are simply different than their neighbors. Isn't that really what Jesus did?

Excellent marketing campaign!

Posted by: Rev. Yates at June 10, 2006 5:53 PM

Rev. Yates, though I certainly agree that "God is love," I would caution that there is more to God than love. He is also just, true, consistent and puts His own glory above everything else. He also clearly condemns homosexuality in scripture. I'm troubled that you do not find this campaign, and their entire website for that matter, in direction opposition to what God clearly outlines in His Word. What, exactly, is excellent about this campaign?

Posted by: Gene Mason at June 11, 2006 1:55 PM

...I know we want to keep it all on marketing, but this is a "church" site, so I'll have to point out to David that although Jesus specifically didn't talk about homosexuality, he covered all the law in Matt 5:18 by saying none of it will pass - we just don't put the hope of our eternal salvation in it.

The big problem is that we seem to have different definitions of love. The UCC believes that with love, you must approve of what they do. I read I Corinthians a few times and can't find that anywhere in there.

But to bring it back to Marketing, I would say **bad marketing** because the twisting of the truth (that being the word of God) is disingenuine. Dishonest marketing will always be exposed by God's truth over time.

Posted by: Matt at June 15, 2006 7:53 AM

Evidently, it wasn't that bad of marketing if it got all of you talking, now is it?

Posted by: Nicki at June 16, 2006 3:56 AM

I would say effective marketing. This campaign has raised the awareness of this issue to the entire population of Indianapolis. From billboards, to print stories, heavy coverage on the TOP25 Market Television stations. Regardless of the morality, humanity, correctness of the message...it has worked to meet the needs of this particular client. If you feel so strongly against the message, then use this VERY EFFECTIVE media campaign to advertise your church's thoughts.

Posted by: Jason at June 16, 2006 9:35 AM

Who said "God Loves Everybody"? Gus you take the lazy way out bye sloughing off everything this campaign is saying bye not actually bothering to study what they are saying as well as making light of it bye proclaiming you know exactly what God meant in every passage of the Bible. Even TRUE biblical scholars are debating this issue.

Posted by: Jason at July 11, 2006 9:29 AM

The campaign is not just about the church. It is about GLBT issues and discrimination. There is a lot more out there to discuss. Unfortunately, Discrimination in the US goes beyond the four walls of any church and the pages of anyone's misread Bible. Our legislative bodies and government halls our overflowing with bigotry and bias. This is just an eye-opener for those who have been sleeping.

Posted by: Terri at July 21, 2006 9:08 PM

Having been raised in the Hate of the Moral Christian Reich. And now a released Nazarene preacher's kid, I praise God there is an attempt to reach others in the dark places. Hate is so easy to throw around, in the name of God; there being too few Christians brave enough to exude God's love and unconditional forgiveness. You may wish to judge my spelling, my life, and my walk with God, remember dear believer "Judge thee not let ye yourself be judged........ten fold?" After you pray are you up to the judgment?

In the Love of the Great I Am.

Posted by: Derrill at December 14, 2006 8:00 PM

I just noticed these signs all over Indy. Having been raised a fundamental Baptist while being a closet lesbian...I am very interested in what they're opinion is but not open to adjusting the word of God either. It has me intrigued at the very least. I read the whole book of Ruth and the story of Jonathan and David during church tonight. I'm not convinced by their chosen examples of Biblical evidence at all. Yet I'm not convinced that I'm bound for Hell because I love the same sex. It's not about religious marketing or church promotion. It comes down to a personal relationship with Jesus that no one can judge or fully understand.

Posted by: Eve at April 29, 2007 8:07 PM [63]

From that one discussion thread alone it is clear that many people were moved to a state of increased awareness and a number of conversations were initiated. Based on that assessment, Phase II of the Campaign in Indianapolis was a huge success. Rev. Jeff Miner provided the following synopsis of media highlights generated during/by the second phase.

- A front-page headline story in the *Indianapolis Star* on April 27 reached several hundred thousand readers, and an on-line dialogue on the *Star* website drew an exceptional number of comments.
- A CBS national news story appeared on LOGO TV.
- Campaign-related TV news stories aired on Channels 6 (ABC), 13 (NBC), and 59 (FOX)—their combined viewership is several hundred thousand. There was a second a follow-up headline story on Channel 6.
- An Indianapolis Christian radio station, 1310 AM, aired two 40-minute radio interviews; shorter interviews were aired on WIBC, Indy's large news-talk radio station, and WFYI,

Indianapolis Public Radio.

- A detailed Associated Press story ran in newspapers like *The Chicago Tribune, The Louisville Courier Journal, The Ft. Wayne Journal Gazette,* and *The South Bend Tribune.*
- A panel discussion and debate involving myself [Rev. Jeff] and a theology professor was held at Wabash College. (Rev. Jeff reported further that the dialogue went very well although the professor was noticeably unprepared, and that the audience's favor shifted palpably in the course of the discussion.)
- *The Chicago Free Press*—Chicago's gay newspaper—ran a cover story proclaiming that gays were finding good news in the Bible via our campaign.
- The campaign was covered in dozens of blogs throughout the United States and Europe.
- The www.wouldjesusdiscriminate.com site experienced heavy traffic—37,000 unique visitors since the campaign began in mid-April 2007.

In large part because of the media attention detailed above, Rev. Jeff believes it likely that more than a million people heard our message of hope and challenge in Phase II. Before Phase III kicked off the week of June 23, 2007, Indy's big news-talk radio station, WIBC, had already interviewed him and run that story.

Each and every day I hear from someone who has something to say about the *Would Jesus Discriminate? Campaign*. When I was in Corporate America, that sort of continuous feedback would have kept me smiling all the way to the bank. In this case, I plan to keep working on the Campaign until there is no more need for it. Should I die before that day comes though, I'll know that campaigners in Indianapolis, in Minneapolis, in Phoenix, in Charlotte, in Dallas, in Tucson, in Florida, in Bath (UK), in Sydney (AU), or maybe someone who just saw a t-shirt or read a sign will continue the effort wherever they are.

I promised to tell you a bit about my story and the path that led me to create the concept for this campaign. So the next chapter is my story.

9
My Story

I began my professional career at age 20, fresh out of college, as a speech pathologist in the Caddo Parish Schools in Louisiana. While serving in the Caddo School for Exceptional Children and the Veterans Administration Hospital in Shreveport, I became intrigued with the emerging application of mainframe computers to the analysis of social services delivery (distribution). (Yes, I confess, I have always been a geek.)

I was fortunate enough to be on a Fellowship supported by a generous patron, and that afforded me the opportunity to design and set up a research project that examined post-discharge patient compliance with recommended therapeutic regimes. My team and I collected data through in-home, out-patient support services, and then tracked readmission rates for those patients. The research and analysis we did then became the foundation for my dissertation (at a later date) and I learned four very important things as a result of that work:

1 Computer technology was going to revolutionize the field of social services.
2 Home-based support services were going to be the next "wave" in health care for chronically disabled or ill patients.
3 Traditional delivery (distribution) systems for health care were highly inefficient, impersonal, disempowering and expensive.
4 Changes in the system were certain to be resisted by social service "long-timers" who were familiar (comfortable) with the current system and by the people who owned the "pipe" for distribution, as well.[64]

Following my work in Louisiana, I spent six more years in the public and private education/rehabilitation sectors in Abilene, Texas. I continued to dabble in computer applications while I worked and had my two children, Joshua and Hannah. I also finished a master's degree and began work on my doctorate.

Later, I divorced and it became essential that I generate more income to support my children. I gathered up the bits and pieces of learning that had come out of my professional work and parlayed them into a business plan for using a new and exciting technology—desktop computers—in the education and rehabilitation fields. I had the good fortune to enter that market at just the right time and the company that I founded took off.

My amazing business partners and our gifted employees had the vision and talent necessary to expand my rudimentary concepts and extend them into several industries, and in 1990, C.H. Love & Company was named in the INC 500 (fastest growing small businesses in America). Also in 1990 I was named among the top 50 young entrepreneurs in the US and was invited to participate in the Birthing of Giants ™ Program jointly organized by the Young Entrepreneurs' Organization, Inc. Magazine, and Massachusetts Institute of Technology.[65] In addition, I served on many not-for-profit boards and the Long Range Technology Committee commissioned by the Texas Education Agency.

From 1990 to 1993, I co-founded several other businesses and as I shared earlier, one of those, Integration Control Systems and Services was acquired by the TORO Company (NYSE:TTC) in 1996. As a part of that acquisition, I went to work for TORO as an executive and was given the assignment of helping bring the TORO distributor network world-wide onto an Internet-enabled customer support system.

When I learned the terminology, I realized that I had been an *early adopter* of Internet technology in several fields including education, rehabilitation, dissemination of public records (New Mexico Information Systems) and transmission of sensor data in oil fields and large-scale irrigation systems.

I got to observe the consumer adoption of the Internet through all of its stages including its entire boom and bust phases in the stock market. As you can imagine, I was by then a confirmed capitalist and a conspicuous consumer, ensconced in "the good life" with all the trappings thereof. My deepest commitment to social change came in the form of writing checks to charities. So, how did I get from the life of a corporate executive to that of a pastor and CEO of Metropolitan Community Churches?

Most of that story will have to wait for another book, but I'll share the basic outline of it with you now. As a result of the teaching I was exposed to as a child and the strong influence of my mother, my maternal grandmother and her family, I am person of faith who carries a bone-deep belief that I am ultimately accountable for any of my own behaviors that may cause another person "to stumble." This book is part of the process of my answering for my own misconceptions and missteps—the prejudices that I still hold, the lies that I still tell, and the resentments that still simmer just below the skin.

Millions of people in America call themselves Christians and they believe that homosexuals cannot be Christians. For 23 years of my life, I believed the same thing, but then I entered a passage of deconstruction that continues to this day.

Let me tell you more about my "passage of deconstruction." I began my theological journey in 1977 while working in an evangelical bus ministry in Shreveport, Louisiana. As part of the ministry, while on a door-knocking campaign in one of the poorest areas of the city, I knocked at the door of a woman's home and invited myself in to visit with her about Jesus Christ.

After presenting the *seven steps of salvation* I asked the woman (I'll call her Etta to protect her privacy), if she was ready to repent, confess, and wash her sins away in baptism. She said she was and we hastened to the church where she was immersed. A white, upper-middle-class audience witnessed the event as Etta, a dirt-poor person of color, who lived in a house with no indoor plumbing and a porch so caved in that access to the front door could only be made across a wooden plank, made her testimony of faith.

On the Sunday following her baptism, Etta, along with her four children, one of whom was an infant in diapers, started riding the church bus to services. I saw the family arrive on the first Sunday, greeted them and helped them find classrooms for Sunday school. I sat with them during the worship service and took them to lunch afterwards.

After a few Sundays, I left Etta and her family to the "care and feeding" of our bus ministry coordinator and I shifted my attention back to finding the next person who needed Good News. A few more weeks into Etta's church attendance, a church nursery worker called Child Protective Services and filed a complaint against Etta. Yes, the upper-middle class, white worker alleged that Etta's poor, black children were victims of neglect and that they did not have adequate clothing, medical care or food.

Those children were removed from their home on the basis of the complaint that church nursery worker filed, and I discovered that the oppression of people of color in that city was so systemic and so entrenched that even my "after the fact" advocacy, in spite of my race, class and education, fell on deaf ears. It took two years for Etta to get her children back! For two years those children were lost to their mother—the whole family trapped in a hell of white superiority—and it was my fault. I drug her into our church and the church dragged her almost to death.

What did Etta do or not do that caused that worker to file the complaint? She lived in poverty. She rode a bus to church where she expected to find a community of Christian people who would love her and welcome her. Instead she found a church whose Jesus apparently discriminated against the poor or people of color or both.

And then there was my divorce. My church did not allow divorced people to teach Sunday school or work in church ministries. Their Jesus discriminated against divorced persons and, by extension, their children. I left the church of my childhood and cast my lot with another literalist church that was "softer" on the divorce issue. Later, I found out that church discriminated against gay people in leadership and women as clergy.

In 1988, when my brother died from complications of AIDS, I hit the issue of discrimination in its most painful manifestation. My brother was gay and he had the disease that my church said was punishment from God for his sin(s). The Jesus of that church discriminated against gay men, people who had AIDS and, as I discovered, their siblings and relatives.

As my brother was dying, my teenage son was watching—he saw how his uncle was treated and he experienced, along with the rest of the family, the "taint" of association. My son, who was realizing that he too was gay, attempted suicide. He saw that his church and his community discriminated against gay people and their families, and he had concluded that Jesus must discriminate as well.

I had told my son that Jesus loved him and that church was a safe, loving space, but then someone moved his Jesus and Joshua couldn't find Him behind the church walls. It was clear that Jesus was inaccessible and boxed up in places where my family just didn't belong any more.

As I shared earlier, I left the Church after that experience and stayed away for ten years. During that decade I "came out" as a lesbian and Sue and I acknowledged to each other our long-term, committed relationship. We joined Exodus Metropolitan Community Church in Abilene, Texas in 1998 and on July 29, 2005, after 25 years in relationship, and 15 years of that "in the closet," we were able to marry in British Columbia.

As I've already mentioned, my post-divorce entry into the business world occurred in 1981. I experienced success, was recognized at the national level for that success, and went on to found several companies. (After all, I wasn't "doing church" so I was able to focus intensely on business.) From 1996 to 2001 I was a corporate executive of the publicly traded TORO Company (NYSE:TTC) and the Chief Operating Officer of an Israeli high-tech venture. Those were the heady times of the Internet-fueled stock market. I had a lot on my mind besides church (and Jesus for that matter!)

While I was working for TORO and for the Israeli technology company, I was interviewed by some of the toughest media people in the industry, including CNBC Squawk. It was through those interviews that I learned a critically important principle:

REV. DR. CINDI LOVE

> Any piece of information can be made to sound
> and look true if the interviewer is prepared to win a
> particular point and the interviewee is not prepared to
> present a strong alternative view. Great interviewers
> and interviewees use the same language, but speak
> from different points of view.

The truth is that first-hand experience of media "whoredom" opened my eyes to the sway of "command and control" religious broadcasting (from the pulpit and the airways) and to the enormous influence it exerts in people's lives and on their attitudes.

I started thinking about Etta again. She had tried to defend her care of her children, but she had been unprepared to counter the view(s) of the System, the Church and an affluent society in which infants always had plenty of formula and diapers readily available.

I reflected on the story of my own divorce. The Elders of my church had asked me if I initiated the divorce because of adultery. Had I said, "Yes," I could have continued as a quasi-member of the community and my husband would have been disfellowshipped (the Church of Christ's equivalent to excommunication.) "No," on the other hand, would have resulted in my being shunned. I knew that the root cause for our divorce was tied up in our failure to bond spiritually as a couple—adultery was but a manifestation of that failure. So, I said, "No, adultery is not the reason for our divorce." I told the truth but I lost my church. I was not (then) prepared to present an alternative view.

I considered the events surrounding my brother's death. My family's unwillingness (or perhaps, inability) to present an alternative view contributed immeasurably to the scope of the tragedy that engulfed us. And finally, I contemplated my own coming out process. The die was cast—I was lesbian and I knew the church I loved would no longer have me. I was also convinced that any alternative view I might offer would be dismissed, so I didn't even make the attempt. And then, I found Metropolitan Community Churches.

And, I found my calling: *to present a strong alternative view.*

Furthermore, I was called to present Jesus' inclusive view that precludes discrimination against any human being. Shortly after that, I decided to seek ordination as a minister in the Metropolitan Community Churches.[66] I wanted to use my skills to reclaim Jesus for my family and for my community.

I came to the Metropolitan Community Churches as the organization was moving away from a US-based structure and opening itself to multi-national, interdependent membership. This is a tough job for the best resourced corporations in the world and a Herculean project for a small, not-for-profit denomination with a controversial "product"—full citizenship for all of its members. As a former executive of the TORO Company, I thought I understood the complexities of helping lead a multi-national corporation fairly well.

Most NYSE companies, though, are not trying to sell the world on the idea that it is okay to be gay and Christian. Even more, they are not trying to convince the world that Jesus was clearly on the side of homosexuals. These are the kinds of "sticky" issues that we generally tried to avoid in the profit-making world.

I started writing this book in January 2005. I was the newly appointed Executive Director of Metropolitan Community Churches, the world's largest and oldest Christian denomination specifically founded on the premise that all people, *including non-heterosexuals,* are the children of God. In two short years as the chief executive of MCC, I have learned more about capitalism than I ever learned at the table of corporate America. I have learned that gay people are very threatening to capitalists. I have learned that a lot of capitalists are televangelists and radio broadcasters in disguise, and I have learned that *media stands in for religion now for many people in America*

Most of all I learned how amazingly brave the people of Metropolitan Community Churches are. For almost 40 years they have worked tirelessly, in the face of endemic discrimination and spiritual violence, to convince an unhearing and unseeing world that the church must be fully inclusive to **really be** the church. They have never given up. Not when their churches were burned to the ground by arsonists; not when lenders and lease holders revoked their loans and leases; not even when they were beaten and killed. In fact, pastors and congregants in 4 of the 24 countries where we operate are currently at risk of death whenever they convene their congregations. It is safe to say that wherever you find oppression based on religious bigotry, you will find MCC *tearing down walls and building up hope.*

It is a great honor to serve among such fiercely tenacious people and to contribute in any way that I can. As a leader in corporate organizations, I learned that we had to be willing to ask ourselves critical questions that ultimately challenged our own core beliefs— if we failed to ask the right questions and make course corrections, too often we missed potentially profitable opportunities. I've found that the same type of probing examination is vital in the church world as well. The important difference is that in this second sphere, failure to ask and act means that people suffer while we sit around on our hands.

To pose the Anglican question, "What would Jesus do?" is a good exercise if you really ask the question and don't just wear the bracelet. While I was a corporate executive, several of my colleagues were members of the 700 Club; they wore those bracelets, and there was a Prayer Warrior team in our plant. I like to believe that those folks worked hard at "being Jesus-like" in their interactions, but only they know for sure.

I never saw any of them discriminate overtly against women,

persons of African descent or Latinos, and I never saw a gay person fired. What I did observe was a subtle, but very real reflection of our society. There was no table designated for the executives in the cafeteria, yet somehow all the white guys ended up eating together—de facto assigned seating. Women were few and far between in the higher tiers of management and non-white people were even scarcer.

What I do know is that the gay, lesbian, bisexual and transgender employees were fearful of the "Jesus freaks" in our company because public professions of faith have become red flags for people who don't play ball in the mainstream. This fear is a tragedy for all of us because it limits our contribution to the world.

I had to turn most of my childhood beliefs inside out to get to the place where this book emerged. Until I started the process of "coming out" as a lesbian, I maintained a mindset that a lot of people were "in my circle" and a whole bunch of others were not. That exclusionary thinking was rooted in my own cultural context—a female US citizen of European descent—and had been fostered by my life experiences as a born again Christian, a capitalist, a successful entrepreneur and a corporate executive. Those self-definitions informed my treatment of the people I encountered in my life—my neighbors, my professional colleagues and my family. Most importantly perhaps, those categorizations determined my treatment of the people I never met at all, but for whom my actions had impact.

In order to accept myself I had to take deep look at everything my role models—my parents, pastors, civic leaders and my teachers—had taught me to believe. When I looked sincerely and carefully, I found that what they'd imparted *was true for them, but not true for me.* And more significantly, I found that a lot of what I had been taught was actually inaccurate.

So, I had to change to be true to myself, and in that process I discovered something better than anything I had experienced in my life as a person of white privilege, as a born again Christian or as a person of means. I discovered the *real Jesus* and that discovery took me out of a corporate office and into living the question, "Would Jesus discriminate?" with my pocketbook and my work. It was both a resurrection experience and a call to action.

Think for a moment about *your* answer to the question "Would Jesus discriminate?" Do *you* need a resurrection experience? Do *you* need a call to action? What did you think and feel when you heard about Matthew Shepard's death? Most of us did nothing— and that's just not acceptable. We are not called to stand silently while an entire community of people is systematically crucified.

Remember how Jesus' words and actions challenged boundaries and included the outcasts. Remember the message recorded in Galatians: "... neither Jew or Greek, ... slave or free, ... all of you are one in Christ Jesus."[67] If you examine the rhetoric of the Christian Right closely, you will see a constant push to drive a wedge between non-heterosexuals and other Americans. As long as non-heterosexuals are perceived to be "different" and "other," denying them access to full civil equality is relatively palatable; but as soon as they are seen to be "like" their fellow citizens, then discrimination and prejudice against them will be revealed as the bigoted, hateful, and un-Christian position that it really is.

The query "Would Jesus discriminate?" is a powerful one. It engages your thoughts regardless of whether or not you are a religious person. I was prompted to consider the question deeply following the national tragedy of 9-11 when I saw a Muslim mother and her child harassed by teenagers in a grocery store. I grieved as the responses around that attack spiraled into violence elsewhere in the world and as ethnic and racial profiling escalated within our own borders. I watched, heartbroken, as people's fear levels fluctuated in reaction to yellow, orange and red threat levels, and hate crimes against all kinds of people—African-Americans, Jews, Muslims and non-heterosexuals—escalated.

We have our work cut out for us.

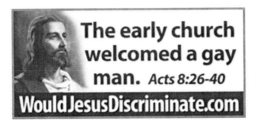

REV. DR. CINDI LOVE

10

We have our Work Cut out for us

Consumer adoption research tells us that it will take 30+ years for an information and education campaign like *Would Jesus Discriminate?* to reach critical mass. We don't have a day to lose. The members of the Christian Right have been working on their campaign to "take back America" since the end of the Cold War. They have a huge head start.

Since 1983 and the production of the film *The Prodigal*, the outreach of the members of the Christian Right through mass media has increased dramatically. *Left Behind: World at War* appeared in churches across the nation and today the producer of *Left Behind* is reviving church film night in communities across America.[68]

Kirk Cameron, one of the stars, says:

> It is something that has never been done before, but
> the idea of creating a distribution system that aims
> to open as many screens as Hollywood's biggest films
> is ingenious. If this works as we all wholeheartedly
> believe it will, then to access the new delivery method,
> Hollywood studios will have to make good family films
> that are acceptable for pastors to show in their churches.
> It is the next step in the process after The Passion.
> This is how we can impact (control) what Hollywood
> produces.[69]

Members of the Christian Right say that "liberals" pick and choose the scriptures that suit them. I submit that members of the Christian Right pick and choose the scriptures that pervert Jesus Christ's call to justice, mercy and compassion. Worse, they pick and choose those scriptures that seem to restrict the universality of God's divine parenthood. This is not the work of Jesus Christ in the world and, therefore, I call upon my brothers and sisters in Christian Right communities the world over to repent of this wrong action and to follow the example of Jesus Christ.

When viewed from the perspective of first century Jewish society, almost everything Jesus did and said can be understood as an indictment of today's fundamentalism. He took to His breast the untouchables at the bottom of the society—the poor, the diseased, the lame, women—why Jesus even ate with "sinners and tax collectors."[70]

When you realize that Jesus befriended those most excluded by Jewish society, that he challenged the cultural mores, and that his every act was seen as rebellious by the religious authorities of the time; it is not hard to understand why the people killed him.

He worked to liberate the most despised people from the

oppression of the legal and social order established in the codes of Leviticus. The idea that Jesus would condemn a non-heterosexual person because of sexual orientation or practices is irreconcilable with the teachings of His words and deeds. If Jesus were physically present with us today, He would invite non-heterosexual people to His table as honored guests.

Either the core of Christianity is the teaching of Jesus or it is not. I believe that Jesus is indeed at the heart of Christianity and, therefore, all the proscriptions of Leviticus are extraneous and their imposition unjustifiable. To condemn a man because of what he is or a woman for some act that is perceived as unclean, is what Jesus preached against. He practiced neither condemnation nor exclusion. In fact, story after story in the New Testament gives demonstration of Jesus' willingness to welcome people, *regardless of the state in which they approached Him.*

Members of the Christian Right in present-day America are trying to re-establish something akin to the ancient legalism of the Pharisees that Jesus so frequently discredited with His words and actions. The *Would Jesus Discriminate? Campaign* provides a useful frame for a political discourse in the religious context of America.

It is time for fair-minded Americans to reset the nation's moral compass to a neutral state in which *all* citizens are afforded the rights of life, liberty and the pursuit of happiness—without discrimination and without prejudice.

Now, let me close this chapter with a listing of scriptures that specifically inform my understanding of Jesus' message. I have chosen just a few as counterpoints to Christian Right's condemnatory citations—I could share hundreds more that say basically the same thing. Please understand, I love the Bible and I love Jesus Christ, and I would never choose to use the example(s) of His life and love in a way that would demean His sacrifice or His truth. He is my exemplar and I have written this book, in part, as an appeal for America's return to the self-evident truths upon which it was founded. It is my earnest prayer and deep desire that we all work toward regarding our neighbors in sacred fidelity.

Scriptures

- I have set you an example that you should do as I have done for you. John 13: 15
- If you really keep the royal law found in Scripture, "Love your neighbor as yourself," you are doing right. James 2: 8.
- If anyone says, "I love God," yet hates his brother, he is a liar. For anyone who does not love his brother, whom he has seen, cannot love God, whom he has not seen. And He has given us this command: Whoever loves God must also love his brother. 1 John 4: 20-21

- For He himself is our peace, who has made the two one and has destroyed the barrier, the dividing wall of hostility… Ephesians 2: 14.
- I have given them the glory that you gave me [Jesus, praying for all believers], that they may be as one as we are one; I in them and you in me. John 17: 22-23.
- Accept one another, then, just as Christ accepted you, in order to bring praise to God. Romans 15: 7
- There is neither Jew nor Greek, slave nor free, male nor female for you [we] are all one in Christ Jesus. Galatians 3:28
- Make room for us in your hearts. We have wronged no one, we have corrupted no one, and we have exploited no one. 2 Corinthians 7: 2

As people of faith, we are called to tear down walls and build up hope.

I understand fear of change and difference, but I also know that fear cannot be overcome by the destruction of "the Other." I understand the members of the Christian Right's disillusionment with a culture which does not easily accommodate the spiritual, but their attempts to reform and theologize society are harming their brothers and sisters and alienating millions from Christ. Their methods lack not only the compassion which is inherent in any real experience of the heart and soul of Jesus Christ, but also the essence of wholeness and goodness that all faiths insist is vital to religious life.

We are trapped in an escalating spiral of hostility and recrimination and we must all hit the reset button; for it is not possible to preach exclusion, hatred and violence from the ineffable center of the Holy Spirit.

11

Hitting the Reset Button

How can we encourage the evolution of new views? I learned a great deal about this process during my time in corporate America and, in particular, during interviews for major television networks. I learned that any statement can be made to function as fact if one party strongly declares it to be so and the other party is not equally vigorous in presenting an alternative aspect. Great interviewers and interviewees use the same language, but speak from different points of view and toward divergent conclusions.

Having that understanding is important for anyone hoping to get any new information, product or service introduced into the American market. We have an information glut here and "talk radio" is the medium of choice for key influencers. Less than 11 percent of the American people read a traditional newspaper.[71]

Over the last fifteen years, more than 90 percent of all radio outlets in the United States have come under the control of the conservative Right. More Americans get their news from FOX than any other outlet.[72] During the same time period, we've seen the polarization of United States of America into "red and blue" zones of competitive, uncompromising rhetoric. We've alienated ourselves from most of the world and lost the respect of millions.

The *Would Jesus Discriminate? Campaign* is designed to produce a clearer understanding of how individuals in varying constituencies and locations ("red" and "blue" states, for example) respond to the issues of discrimination, inequality, exclusion, and the escalation of hate crimes against non-heterosexuals that mark us today. The Campaign entails exchanges between people representing all walks of life—from secular and faith-based organizations as well as from the many communities in America.

I believe that this interaction will make it possible for us to start a new dialogue in America. Out of that dialogue, I hope that we can develop a kind of fair-minded and constitutionally conforming framework and agenda that, in turn, will support effective social action by our citizens.

Although our collective foundation is solid, we need a face lift. We've allowed ideologues to distract us from the routine condition assessments and rigorous maintenance functions that our democratic system requires. Because of that, our culture is awash with poisons—extremism and exclusion, hatred and intolerance, violence and fear. These toxins are tearing us apart and, at the same time, eating away at the very fabric of all that has been good about America. We are tolerating a methodical dismantling of our egalitarian, democratic system and we are handing a mess to our children and grandchildren.

Some of our youth are already living with the effects of our dysfunction. Let me give you an example:

> Anthony Hergesheimer, 15, was walking home from school in Pueblo, Colorado on April 5 (2007) when a group of schoolmates peppered him with disparaging remarks about his openly gay lifestyle and then hurled an aerosol can that struck him in the nose. Hergesheimer suffered a fractured cheekbone and was required to undergo surgery for a broken nose and other facial injuries. A total of six high school students have been charged in the attack which was motivated by nothing more than Hergesheimer's gayness. Two of the students face felony charges of second-degree assault and committing a bias-motivated crime; the other four face juvenile charges.[73]

Unless we want to see this type of situation repeated again and again in our country, we need to demonstrate to our children that it is unacceptable to harm a fellow citizen because of his or her characteristics. We need to reaffirm our core values of peaceful coexistence and cooperation.

Religion best serves our nation and each of us individually, not as an ideology but as a faith structure. It is rightly the source of compassion, a comforting presence, a prophetic voice, a call to our best selves and an inspiration for helping the most vulnerable and marginalized among us. The values most significant to all of us living together in this country are those that promote both the common good and a healthy, peaceful future for the generations to come—not those that seek to establish the sectarian morality of one particular religious or political group.

As citizens, we should care deeply about strengthening our democratic principles for they have served us well even in our most imperfect moments. We should care deeply about strengthening our national commitment to religious freedom rather than feeling threatened by a multiplicity of faiths. We should also care deeply about true integrity in our framing and pursuit of the American dream. If that dream is increasingly unattainable to the majority of our citizens and if only the religiously orthodox are afforded full freedom and all the blessings of democracy, then we are losing our intrinsic "American-ness."

I believe that we face an incipient theocracy in the United States today in that our officials are, ever more frequently, claiming divine sanction or precedent for their pronouncements and policies. My great-great grandparents escaped from countries where their religious practice was no longer tolerated. They would be appalled by the escalating presence of religion in the halls of state.

Don't get me wrong. They would pray for our leaders to follow God's will and to be blessed with wisdom; but they would fight to preserve the separation of church and state. More and more often, religion is being used in the United States as a tool to influence policy and advance political strategy. And, more and more, one voice is taking precedence over another.

The common values of the American people are being replaced by standards that serve particular and specialized interests. Religion no longer elicits respect nor facilitates understanding among vastly diverse groups—religion is being wielded as a political implement and its powerful unifying force is being severely compromised.[74]

I have become uneasy with what I see as the increasingly theocratic nature of my government and I think most Americans share that view. In order to prevent the inevitably negative consequences of that trend though, we need to ask the right questions of our leaders and of ourselves. If we don't, our nation will repeat horrible mistakes of the past. In fact, we're already doing so.

REV. DR. CINDI LOVE

Many of our current leaders, both religious and political figures, say that the United States of America is a Christian nation. Any of you reading this book who believe this is true will want to support the *Would Jesus Discriminate? Campaign* and its partner initiative, the *Faith in America Campaign.* These nationwide educational campaigns will help you, your pastors and priests, neighbors and co-workers to focus clearly on the steps required to create an atmosphere in which the life and example of Jesus Christ are central to societal interactions. Notice, I did not say "…in which the Christians are in control." Indeed, Jesus was no "control-monger" and I believe that the people who try to use His authority and words as instruments of control are not following His example.

The *Would Jesus Discriminate? Campaign* walks us through some history as well as through current realities so we can test the America we know today against the ideal of a "Christian nation." If we are to be a genuinely Christian nation, then we have no choice but to adopt the words and deeds of Jesus Christ as the core truths of our national ethos.

In fact, you can check the standards for yourself in less than one hour. Go to the Internet and type in the URL "www.bible.com". Type "Jesus" into the search engine there, and you'll be presented with a complete listing of every (recorded) word Jesus spoke and every action He took during both His life on earth and the brief period of return after His resurrection from the dead.

I like to start at the end of the list with the account of Jesus saying to Peter, "feed my sheep" and later "Follow me!" When I was growing up, I heard very few interpretations of that text—I don't think anyone ever told me that Jesus was speaking of Peter's martyrdom in the passage. Indeed, if you read it, you will see that Jesus grilled Peter thoroughly about the authenticity and strength of his love for Jesus. He predicted Peter's death, and then handed the leadership of an entire community of believers to Peter with the simple statement "Follow Me." For Peter to follow Jesus he would have to lead the disciples—and the ultimate price of that following and leading was to be his own death.

I also appreciate Luke's narrative of Jesus hanging on the cross between the two thieves who squabbled across Him about His identity and His power—if Jesus were the real Son of God, why didn't He just get down off the cross (and save the criminals while He was at it!)? Instead of saving Himself though, Jesus, close to death, promises one of the men hanging there with Him that they'll be together in paradise later that day. When I was a child, this made no sense to me.

My church drilled the *seven steps of salvation* (including "... repent and be baptized...") into me and I spent a fair amount of time in fear of dying suddenly in some accident and having no last chance to beg God for forgiveness. I asked an Elder in my church about this apparent dichotomy—how could the thief join Jesus if he had not repented and been baptized? I was told that the man had repented, but I couldn't find any scriptural support for that claim. When I asked about the baptism part I got a vague response along the lines of "Well, Jesus made an exception." Then I had to wonder how it was that Elder was able to read just a little bit more into his Bible than I could into mine and whether Jesus might still be in the business of granting exceptions to ordinary sinners.

What I believe is that there is no need for exceptions and no need to "add to or take away from" what we read in Scripture about Jesus. In particular, Jesus made no mention of homosexuality, so how (or why) did the modern Church pick up the issue as a central theme for the 21st century? Jesus did mention a lot of other things and, in fact, He got angry about some things—a barren fig tree, money changers in the table, impulsive Peter cutting off the ear of a guard—but of harsh pronouncements regarding non-heterosexuals … not a word from the mouth of Jesus.

We've really messed things up in the Christian church and in this so-called Christian nation. We need to ask ourselves, "Would Jesus discriminate?"

I believe we will know that we are truly a Christ-centered nation when our behaviors are modeled on His behaviors. Jesus did not oppress women—neither should we. Jesus did not discriminate against people of different races or religions—neither should we. In fact, Jesus specifically *in*cluded people who were not a part of His religious or ethnic communities, and we can be successful as a truly Jesus-centered nation only when we no longer *ex*clude people of color and people who do not identify as Christian.

We can be a truly Christ-centered nation when we no longer allow our own homophobia—our irrational fear of lesbian, gay, bisexual and transgender people—to stop us from doing what is really right. Jesus would have included non-heterosexual people at the table with Him as disciples and indeed, there are hundreds of thousands of them serving as His disciples today.

Let me repeat an absolute truth: Jesus never mentioned homosexuality. Furthermore, the six or seven Bible passages typically used to justify the exclusion of non-heterosexuals have been misinterpreted and misapplied just as surely as the verses used by the Church to defend slavery, segregation and the oppression of women were misinterpreted and misapplied. We were smart enough to recognize our errors around the issues of (traditional) civil rights and women's rights, and we are astute enough to stop discrimination against non-heterosexuals as well.

People who disagree with me will say that I "pick and choose" scriptures to suit my own perspective. Clearly, we all do this or we would still be stoning women to death for adultery and no one would be divorced. The question is whether the Bible was intended to guide us into more loving relationships with God and one another or whether it was intended to leave us stranded and separate from God and one another. Fundamentalism deprives us of intelligent and compassionate relationship with one another, and I find no evidence in the life of Jesus Christ to support its practice.

I regret that we are far off the mark of ideal Christianity today. More than 100 million Christian congregants are being instructed by their faith leaders that the exclusion of non-heterosexual people from full communion with Christ and His Church is scripturally justifiable and thus appropriate. The job of faith and political leaders (as I understand it) is to guide people toward mercy, love and justice. Furthermore, we should lead with mercy, love and justice so as to repair the world, not fracture it.

The majority of us stand by while non-heterosexuals face curtailed rights and even abuse in the workplace, in our schools and in our churches. Most of our government officials were reluctant even to enhance existing hate crimes legislation in order to protect homosexuals and the disabled from unwarranted attacks. Why?

Probably because most of us don't call them up and say "We care. Do what's right. Let's remember history and not repeat the mistakes of the past." I commend our partners, the Human Rights Campaign, The Y. A. Flunder Foundation, New Dimensions Worship Center & Bishop Carlton Pearson, The Task Force, LAMDA Legal, GLAAD, GLSEN and Faith in America,[75] for trying to bring us to the center of what we really need to do as a nation.

I really believe that Jesus would challenge us to repent if He were here today because we are missing the mark. I think most of us have placed moral brackets or blinders around our lives and we can't (or don't choose to) hear truth that is inconsistent with our core beliefs, at least not until those core beliefs are directly addressed and reshaped. Too many of us are asleep at the wheel because we think it doesn't matter what happens to a "bunch of faggots or people on welfare who ought to get up and work for a living" (a direct quote from one of my former in-laws). I think we need to examine our core beliefs.

Do we really believe in freedom and democracy and equal protection under the law? What happens if we fail to defend these basic principles? We know what happened with the indigenous people of the continental US—they were slaughtered. We know what happened to Japanese-Americans during WWII—they were rousted from their homes and put into internment camps in their own country. We know what happened to people of color—they were enslaved, beaten and lynched, and later subjected to Jim Crow legislation designed to maintain their marginalization.

Women have faced oppression as well and even now it appears that some members of the Christian Right and literalist churches are still advocating that women be "submissive." Hard to believe, but true. Is this what we want for our children and grandchildren? Where the church leads, society follows. Think about it.

We practice moral bracketing to a great degree in this country, and it offers us a convenient and psychologically comfortable way to get by with murder and violence against innocent people. Hitler did it his way. Now we Americans are doing it in a whole new way.

Non-heterosexuals are the "new" Jews, the "new" Blacks and the "new" Latinos. Although some people of color resent the comparison of racism to heterosexism, the simple fact is that no one is free while one is not free. We know this in our collective gut and yet we are still standing by. We don't want to get into the fray. We don't want to dispute the accepted authorities. We want to get along, so we go along.

Now again, before you think I am preaching to you, let me remind you that I was responsible for spiritual violence against my own brother, Patrick. I dedicated this book to him for that reason.

You'll remember from an earlier chapter that Patrick was gay. When he came out, I joined the rest of my family in rejecting him. We did not want him to come home for holidays if he brought his "partner" and we did not want him to tell anyone else that he was gay. When Patrick contracted AIDS in 1988, we brought him home to die and lied about his illness. We told people he had cancer. We were so afraid of what our neighbors would think of us that we let our own brother/son/uncle go to his grave thinking we were ashamed of him. Part of the reason I wrote this book is to help right that wrong.

What makes it okay for any of us to reject members of our own families? Or for that matter, what about rejecting our neighbors or perfect strangers—is that right? Who said so? Why do we believe what we do? Do we believe what our parents told us? Can we be sure our parents were right? Do you believe because the Pastors say so? Are you sure that they're right? Maybe you believe because the President says so. Are you certain he's right? Do you believe because the Bible says so? Do you know what it really says?

If you call yourself a Christian, these questions can be particularly problematic because you must hold yourself to the "Jesus Standard." *Do unto others as you would have them do unto you. Love God with all your heart, soul and mind and your neighbor as yourself.*

Yet those of us who claim Christianity for ourselves and our country systematically deconstruct legal protections for non-heterosexuals (and for women.) "No way!" you say, "I don't do that." But consider please: we are, in our unthinking consumerism, complicit in the command and control of the media by members of the Christian Right. We watch their channels, we listen to their radio broadcasts, and we read their newspapers. In short, we buy into their success with our own information intake.

Remember that the majority of all radio distribution is

REV. DR. CINDI LOVE

controlled by the Right. Over the past 15 years independent investigative reporters—the folks who do the tedious work of researching and exposing illegal and unjust activities—have been less and less able to access airtime for their work; instead of picking up free-lancers' features, the major distributors broadcast the stories they've assigned their own journalists to cover.[76] Ouch, how did that happen, and is that a situation we're comfortable with? Do we really want that huge chunk of broadcast information coming to us pre-screened through a single filter?

We may not be able to do anything about the information coming at us, but we can certainly claim and use our own filters. And the truth is we all *need* some kind of standard against which to assess the events in our lives. Where do we stand on what is happening in our neighborhoods and in our workplaces? What criteria do we use in making these decisions? For my yardstick and measure, I have chosen one of the world's greatest historical leaders of social change—the individual I call my personal Savior,[77] Jesus the Christ—and I use the question "Would Jesus discriminate?" as my filter.

Asking the question of someone you know is a simple exercise; you needn't be afraid of the answers you might get or any truth(s) that might arise out of your conversations. Whether we choose to acknowledge it or not, each of us has a deep well of love and trust to access. Frankly, I trust my neighbor a lot more than I do most of our world leaders right now. I may not even know my neighbor, but I know the world leaders—I'll take a chance on my neighbors.

By asking the question, you can create an opportunity for dialogue. You can talk about the history of the Bible, how people of faith have used the Book to support segregation, and how those people really and truly thought they were right at the time. But then Martin Luther King, Jr. presented an alternative view, and strong people of faith led their congregations, their communities and their families to deeper study and understanding.

Today, segregation is not condoned by any mainstream religious denomination. Churches repented of the mean-spirited and harmful behaviors of segregation and we can repent again! In fact, I believe that we *will* repent again, and that the catalyst for change this time may well be the frequent repetition of the simple question, "Would Jesus discriminate?"

12

Moving Beyond the Mistakes

Remembering past discrimination provides us with the "take home" lesson that we need to avoid the mistakes of prior generations. Mistaken ideas have led good people to do bad things. As recently as February 2007, in Detroit, Michigan, a fellow passenger on a city bus asked 72-year-old Andrew Anthos if he was gay. The passenger then followed Mr. Anthos off the bus, attacked him with a metal pipe and fled. Mr. Anthos died from his injuries; according to media reports, police are continuing the investigation without any solid leads.

On February 19, 1999, in Sylacauga, Alabama, 39-year old computer programmer Billy Jack Gaither, was brutally beaten with an ax handle. His throat was cut, and his body was set on fire. One of his convicted killers, Steven Mullins, testified he killed Gaither because he was "queer."

In October of 1998, Matthew Shepard encountered Russell Henderson and Aaron McKinney inside the Fireside Bar in Laramie, Wyoming; he left with them and the three men traveled in a pickup truck to the edge of town. Henderson tied Shepard to a rail fence and McKinney beat him with a.357 Magnum. They took his shoes and wallet, intending to rob his apartment, but returned to town and got into a fight with 2 other young men. Police picked Henderson up in the aftermath of that fight and collected a bloody gun, along with other evidence, but were not aware, at the time, of the earlier crime. A passing cyclist discovered Matthew hanging on the fence the next day—he had been tied there for about 18 hours. He never regained consciousness and died several days later.

Although consistently fewer than 10,000 hate crimes per year (in the USA) have been officially documented, a 2005 report from the Bureau of Justice Statistics suggests the true number is likely closer to 191,000.[78] According to the Southern Poverty Law Center's Intelligence Project, this means the real level of hate crimes likely runs between 19 and 31 times what has been officially reported for the past 15 years.[79]

Why have gays become the target of such brutality? What is the source of this kind of hatred?

The answer is simple. Citizens of the most democratic nation in the world believe that discrimination against non-heterosexual people—individually and as a group—is okay. It is a sanctioned behavior and changing it is something our parents, schools, churches and media have generally done little to promote. Clearly, we must teach ourselves and our children to self-monitor, to regulate and to alter traditional mindsets, or the discrimination will continue unchecked and its consequences will not only persist but escalate.

REV. DR. CINDI LOVE

Jesus told us that whatever we do to the least of people, we do to Him. Will we leave Jesus hanging on that rough fence?

Today, the simple question "Would Jesus discriminate?" serves as a filter for my theology and my citizenship. I see no evidence that He discriminated against anyone—rather the contrary. As He moved from place to place, He gathered people from the edges and He drew close to the people most excluded by society. In Jesus' three years of activism and ministry, He embraced all as His siblings, and left behind two major instructions: Love God, and love your neighbor as yourself. And that last, of course, begs the question, "Who is my neighbor?"

The next steps toward change are critical and will require that progressive, secular organizations adapt significantly and collaborate meaningfully with spiritually focused concerns. The issues and concerns of religious leaders must be incorporated into progressive agendas, and they must be enabled to speak their *in their own voices* for social change. Historically, religious organizations have been committed to cultural transformation. By considering and applying their approach to this commitment, the progressive movement today might well achieve more than the merely formal victories of litigation and legislation—it could produce powerful new strategies for making justice a reality in people's daily lives.

13

Getting Real

If we want to "get real" in America we have to start with ourselves. It is up to all of us to "get real" enough to deconstruct our religious, socio-cultural and familial blueprints to those heart spaces where the truth rests in each of us—those places where we can admit to our own deeply ingrained but externally invisible prejudices.

I had an experience recently that really speaks to this issue of deeply-seated but largely invisible prejudice. In my hometown[80] on May 3, 2007, the National Day of Prayer,[81] there were two separate and distinct public prayer meetings. One group, almost exclusively Christian (and largely Church of Christ and Southern Baptist Convention members,) met on the steps of City Hall and was welcomed there by the Mayor, himself a member of the Church of Christ. The local Interfaith Council had applied to provide representative prayers from non-Christian faiths (specifically Buddhist, Hindu, Jewish and Unitarian) at that assembly, but when their request was denied an alternative prayer meeting was organized. The second group gathered in a nearby public park, where their assembly was allowed, but not sanctioned, by the city government.

In a country that is often divided over the question of prayer in school, we couldn't make room for the prayers of all of the people who wanted to meet on the steps of City Hall. Not even on the National Day of Prayer. What a tragedy!

I was further disappointed when I learned that the National Day of Prayer Task Force, a private organization headed by Shirley Dobson (the wife of Focus on the Family's Dr. James Dobson) had effectively co-opted the national observance, going so far as to include the phrase "Official Website" in its own banner headline[82] and to claim for itself not only the title "NDP headquarters" but also the function of "official 'clearinghouse' for all position statements."[83] How ironic! Focus on the Family pushes the issue of prayer in the public school, arguing, in effect, that prayer is appropriate, if not essential, for all children, regardless of their religious affiliation. But only representatives of the "Judeo-Christian tradition" are welcome to participate in "official" National Day of Prayer events.

This isn't right for America. If you can answer the question "Would Jesus discriminate?" from the perspective of Jesus' teachings (or those of your preferred prophet,) then you'll be able to think clearly about social dynamics in America and the world. You'll be better able to assess what you ought to do, how you fit into the larger stream of events, and what your responsibilities are not only to your family and your community but to the future as it unfolds.

The United States has a long-standing tradition of citizen action and that's the tradition and action that I, through Metropolitan Community Churches, am engaged in now. Many of you reading this book undoubtedly belong to a church and/or one or more volunteer-based organizations. You can help make a difference on your own as a citizen/member and through those groups as well. If we make this commitment together, then we can deal with almost anything—health care, the economy, security diplomacy. We can bring a broken world together and create for all of the world's children the future they deserve, by bending that world toward survival and justice rather than destruction and ruin.

The members of the Christian Right believe that they are trying to "reclaim" a Christian society. Abraham Foxman, national director of the Anti-Defamation League, in a November 3, 2005 speech said:

> Make no mistake: We are facing an emerging Christian right leadership that intends to 'Christianize' all aspects of American life, from the halls of government to the libraries, to the movies, to recording studios, to the playing fields and local rooms of professional, collegiate and amateur sport, from the military to Sponge Bob Square Pants.[84]

We ("my team") argue that setting the standards for American society is not the purview of one group, no matter how altruistic their intentions; and furthermore, that the methods of the Right are not only inherently harmful to non-heterosexual people, but also intrinsically "un-Jesus-like."

> The Christian Right has attacked the rights of women as well as gay men and lesbians in a concerted effort to impose their theological views on the secular body politic—and the bodies of millions of people in our

society ... [For many Americans who are challenging the Christian Right, t]he issue is not secular belief versus spiritual faith; the issue is how to craft a pluralist civil society that honors the dignity of both secular philosophy and spiritual faith, while insisting that theological claims alone should never dictate public policies. That's why we say we are challenging theocracy; because that's what the Christian Right is increasingly sowing: a theocratic society.[85]

What can you do if you don't want that kind of society? Lobby for anti-discrimination laws in your communities. If you pray, please pray for enlightenment among the people who encourage spiritual violence against non-heterosexual people. Pray for people like Joni Lamb, the co-founder of the Daystar Network.

Several years ago, I was asked to appear on a live program[86] with Joni. That experience convicted me of the necessity for broader dissemination of information about the way that Jesus really interacted with people who were from the margins of society. It also convinced me that more people like me need to interact with more people like Joni.

Even though Joni said that the reason she asked me on the show was to learn how better to minister to people like me, it was clear that another agenda was in play. I don't think she intentionally seeks to harm gay people, but her ministry is indeed hurtful—it was a tough interview.

Both of us had extensive media experience and both of us had a particular view on the subject. She used all of the techniques of a sophisticated interviewer in an attempt to move me to a position of "confessing" that my sexuality makes me unhappy or interferes with my ministry. She tried guilt. She tried an appeal to my "call" as a minister. She tried appeals to virtually all aspects of my humanity in order to "win" her point in the interview. She is

REV. DR. CINDI LOVE

very intelligent and a gifted interviewer (I would be very pleased to welcome her to our team) and she knows how to maneuver the interviewee into a position of vulnerability.

Joni asked me about my divorce from my husband and told me that God does not like divorce. She related to me that she had done a series of interviews with men "drawn into the homosexual lifestyle" and told me how unhappy all those men were. She said that she has interviewed hundreds of people who have "come out" of homosexuality, and that there is no way around the scripturally supported fact that God does not intend for people to be gay. She said, "You really cannot reconcile homosexuality and the Bible."

Fortunately, I was given great media training and experiences in my corporate past, and I think I held my own with her. I told her that I am made in God's image, that there is no condemnation for people who believe and accept Jesus Christ in their lives. I reminded her that neither one of us, women, would be accepted as ministers today if the literal interpretation of Scripture still prevailed in our society. I also reminded her that Scripture has been used to justify both slavery and racism.

As we neared the end of the interview, she pulled out the Jesus followers' "big gun": she asked if Jesus were to appear to me in the flesh *right now*, say that He loves me and accepts me, and then ask me to give up homosexuality; would I do so. My response was that Jesus *is* living with me right now and He hasn't asked me to give up homosexuality.

At the end of the interview, she announced, "I can't compromise what I know to be truth and I have so many testimonies of people—I've never met a person involved in this lifestyle who is happy and has true peace." I was delighted to let her know that she *was in luck that day because I was (and remain!) happy and at peace.* I told her that I have accepted what I am promised by the indwelling of the Holy Spirit. She ended the interview at that point. Later, when I was writing this chapter and wanted to view excerpts of that interview, I searched the Joni Show archives and also used a powerful global search engine. I was unable to find even a mention of the taping—apparently I've been erased!

People like Joni and groups like Exodus International[87] stand to lose a lot of income if non-heterosexuals are really okay with God, particularly if they don't have another card to play in the media. To avoid that possibility, they have expanded their efforts in recent months and have launched additional offensives (pun intended) in their war on homosexuality.

A report by the Task Force Policy Institute, *Youth in the Crosshairs: the Third Wave of Ex-Gay Activism,* found that

> Ex-gay programs and their evangelical Christian Right allies are focusing less on"curing" adults of homosexuality and more on preventing its development by targeting parents, children and adolescents…ex-gay programs are recommending that parents commit their children to treatment of "prehomosexuality" even if it is against their children's wishes. Heterosexual youth are also being recruited in schools and churches to spread the message that homosexuality is a treatable mental illness.
>
> One of the most disturbing accounts…a 5-year-old boy who was subjected to conversion therapy to address "prehomosexuality"…"involves a psychologist who claims that his theories and treatments are scientific," said study co-author Jason Cianciotto, the Policy Institute's research director. "To the contrary, conversion therapy is opposed by nearly every medical and mental health professional association, including the American Academy of Pediatrics."
>
> He added, "Studies cited by ex-gay leaders to support

their claims suffer from fatal methodological flaws, and are contradicted by respected, peer-reviewed academic research. Tragically, ex-gay and evangelical Christian Right leaders are using bogus theories and discredited research to frighten parents into doing something more likely to harm than help their children." [88]

The *Would Jesus Discriminate? Campaign* offers an alternative view—a competing narrative—to that of the Christian Right. The campaign teaches people facts about the Bible including the specific item that Jesus never mentioned homosexuality. It also teaches people that it is wrong to exclude non-heterosexual people from full citizenship in the Beloved Community of God. I have a dream that one day people like Joni and the ex-gay activists in Exodus International will reverse their positions and devote their considerable resources and talents to repairing the harm that has resulted from their investment in spiritual violence.

Now, you can see the challenge that we have. We have to rehabilitate the Christian Right and cure their disease of rejection. I trust in the Great Physician and that faith informs my knowledge that we can be healed. It is possible for us to live as neighbors in this country.

Getting the right people on our team will hinge on being able to include media networks and media professionals to present our views, not in exclusion of, but in addition to those of the Christian Right. We have to create enough "buzz" to make media outlets want to pick up our stories. Then, we have to sustain the story lines in such a way that more viewers/listeners tune into those outlets. More viewers will result in those outlets being able to pull in more advertising dollars; more advertising dollars mean greater profit; and if our stories help them make a profit, the various information purveyors will certainly carry those stories.

Give that some thought if you influence the purchase of

television or other advertising. Think about it when you tune in to your favorite shows and particularly if you live in the United States. We've all but turned media into religion here and our influence extends to every part of the globe. Just a gentle reminder: we are still the world's "opinion leaders"—our words and actions are closely monitored everywhere and weigh heavily in decisions and policies elsewhere. As leaders, we must be conscious of and accountable for the behaviors we engage in and the examples we set.

In the last year, Metropolitan Community Church has been at the forefront of resistance against hate-crimes and violence committed against non-heterosexual people in Jamaica and Eastern Europe. Those places may seem far removed to you, but the inhabitants there are no less our neighbors because of any distance. I want to take this opportunity to "enlist" your spirit where shocking physical violence occurs[89] (and is sometimes overlooked, if not condoned, by legal authorities.)

Conclusion

Are there any still Rejected by Christ?

Non-heterosexuals are rejected by most people—let's start and end this book with them. Some Christians say that homosexuals (and other non-heterosexuals) are rejected by Christ; they sometimes attempt to soften their indictment with statements like "Love the sinner, hate the sin."

In my lifetime, I have met many Christians who believe that non-heterosexuals are not the beloved children of God. My denomination, Metropolitan Community Churches, has provided funerals for thousands of individuals whose family churches refused to bury them due to their identification as gay people or because their deaths resulted from AIDS. As I have ministered to the bereaved friends and families, I have often seen Jesus.

The image which most often comes to me is similar to the final scene in the movie *Places in the Heart*. The murdered husband and his African-American killer appear in the church pews together, reconciled by that peace which passes all understanding, the love of Jesus Christ. In my musing, the recently departed (usually a gay man) joins the movie characters, and Jesus sits there with all of them. Everyone smiles.

I am holding on to this mental picture and smiling as I conclude this book. I am holding on to my hope that many of you can see yourselves in that picture as well—at peace and smiling.

Appendix I

Some Early Experiences

I had my first major chance to test the model for diffusion of innovation while working with the introduction of a consumer robotics product in the United States. I was privileged to work with Dr. Trichy Krishnan[90] at Rice University in the development and testing of a model to accelerate adoption of a robotic lawnmower. Alas, the research clearly indicated that it was a product "ahead of its time" except for the bravest of early adopters.

I used a variation of this model to design a concept for the Visiting Investigator program at NASA in the mid-nineties. That concept involved the use of sensor technology to predict the deterioration of water supplies due to chemical intrusion. We hoped to convince industrialists to adopt the sensor technology to minimize release of pollutants into streams. The industrialists were not early adopters either.

I learned a great deal through these experiences and ultimately applied the model in a successful venture that I sold to The TORO Company (NYSE: TTC) in 1996. The innovation, later dubbed The TORO National Support Network (www.toro.com), revolutionized the way in which golf course superintendents were supported in their goal of never missing a watering window on the links (too much lost playing time equaled lost revenues!) In that case, the communication of the concept through certain channels, over a certain time period, and among a particular group of customers proved successful. TORO national sales force personnel, TORO Distributors, TORO product specifiers and architects served as the communications channels and, of course, golf course superintendents were the target consumers.

Today more than 15,000 golf course superintendents use some form of that innovation that we developed at Integration Control Systems & Services (ICSS, Inc.), and the S-shaped diffusion curve, first mapped over 100 years ago, is visible in the logo of The TORO National Support Network. That curve was also a graphic symbol for Phil Walter's (TORO's Director of Golf Irrigation) favorite race track at the time.

Appendix II

Faith in America's Campaigns

The following information regarding Faith in America's campaigns is taken from The Faith in America (www.faithinamerica.com) website. The initialism LGBT is used for Lesbian, Gay, Bisexual and Transgender.

- The world's great religious traditions practiced within the United States of America emphasize love of neighbor as well as love of God. Compassion, justice, freedom, and respect for the dignity of all people are their most authentic and noble expressions. However, in the United States, lesbian, gay, bisexual and transgender people are victims of religious teachings based on ignorance and fear.

- This abuse of Religion influences all aspects of public life in

America, including civil laws and social attitudes. Because of it, lesbian, gay, bisexual and transgender people are denied equal rights and protection under civil law. They are discriminated against and socially ostracized. Physical violence against them is incited.

- This expression of religion-based bigotry against lesbian, gay, bisexual, and transgender people has historical precedents, including violence, intolerance, and inequity toward women, people of color, and people with religious traditions different from those of the majority, such as Jews, Roman Catholics, Mormons and others. These precedents are recognized today by the mainstream of America to have been misguided, wrong and evil.

- To end the persecution of gay people engendered by religion-based bigotry, its common link with these historical precedents must be acknowledged. Faith in America, Inc. is confident that, just as Americans have rejected the distorted religious teachings that sanctioned these injustices, Americans will reject the religion-based bigotry against lesbian, gay, bisexual, and transgender people when it is exposed.

THE 2006 FAITH IN AMERICA CAMPAIGNS

In 2006, Faith In America, Inc. initiated media campaigns in the following locations. Each campaign addressed the misuse of religion to justify discrimination against lesbian, gay, bisexual and transgender people.

BALTIMORE, MARYLAND

In January, 2006, Faith In America, Inc. collaborated with the National Black Justice Coalition. During the Senate hearing regarding the Supreme Court nomination of Samuel Alito, Faith In America paid for the creation and publication of an ad that

NBJC sponsored in Roll Call, the Congressional daily newspaper, and in two Afro-American weekly newspapers in the Baltimore/Washington area. The ad compared the lack of marriage equality for same-gender couples to anti-interracial marriage laws that were abolished by the US Supreme Court ruling in *Loving vs. Virginia*, June 12, 1967. As a consequence, Alexander Robinson, NBJC's President and CEO, was interviewed about the ad and marriage equality for same-gender couples on the MSNBC Tucker Carlson Show.

In May and June, 2006, Faith In America again collaborated with the National Black Justice Coalition in a four-week long ad campaign. Faith In America paid for the creation and publication of four ads that were sponsored by NBJC in the Afro-American weekly newspapers. This campaign promoted NBJC's First Annual Faithful Call To Justice, a national observance held in black churches around the nation on June 24-25, 2006. The events on this day focused on the inclusion of openly gay people in faith communities, support for marriage equality and the spiritual harm of homophobia.

Polls were conducted before and following the ad campaign to measure the impact of the ads on attitudes toward gay people.

HICKORY/TAYLORSVILLE, NORTH CAROLINA

The Mitchell Gold + Bob Williams factory is located in Taylorsville, North Carolina, a small town a short distance from Hickory, one of the larger cities in the area. It was important to Faith In America's founder Mitchell Gold to conduct media campaigns in Hickory and Taylorsville if he was going to conducting them in other places in the United States. Before we initiated the campaign here, Mitchell mailed a personal letter to each of his 750 employees explaining the mission of Faith In America and alerting them to the upcoming campaigns. This was an act of integrity on Mitchell's part. In May and June, ads challenging religion-based bigotry were published in the Hickory and Taylorsville newspapers. As a result, a steady mix of critical and supportive letters was published in the newspapers responding to the ads. The local Baptist Association and a local Church of Christ congregation published full-page ads denouncing the Faith In America ads. Also, in response to the ad campaign, the local Baptist Association sponsored a Sunday night rally open to the public at which a "former homosexual" preacher spoke. Mitchell and Jimmy Creech, Executive Director of Faith In America, attended. Following the rally, Mitchell and Jimmy engaged the speaker and the head of the Baptist association in civil and promising dialogue.

Prior to and following the campaigns, polling was done to determine the impact of the media campaigns. There was no discernable difference in the pre- and post-campaign polls. However, the positive news is that the media campaign did not produce negative results or backlash. Also, a very public conversation has been initiated about homosexuality and religion. We have received many letters and emails of support. We believe it is important to continue the campaign to create measurable positive indicators that attitudes have changed.

Faith In America rented billboards on Interstate 40 (heavily traveled by residents of Taylorsville and Hickory) that read: "Religion-Based Bigotry – Let's End It Now"; and, "Religion-Based Bigotry Is Bad Religion." The FIA Web site was featured on each billboard. These billboards will continue to challenge of religion-based bigotry through mid-April, 2007.

Mitchell and Jimmy have been hosting breakfast meetings of two to three supportive clergy at a time in Hickory and Taylorsville. Out of these meetings, a core of fifteen clergy has been developed which will provide the foundation for a community-wide event to be held in Hickory in January or February, 2007. Our objective is to host a gathering of 200 to 300 people for an open and informed dialogue about the history of religion-based bigotry and the current misuse of religion to deny gay people the full rights and protections guaranteed by the US Constitution.

GREENSBORO, NORTH CAROLINA

In June, 2006, the Southern Baptist Convention met in Greensboro, North Carolina. In collaboration with the Triad Equality Alliance – an organization based in the Greensboro, Winston-Salem and High Point area which advocates for civil rights for lesbian, gay, bisexual and transgender people, Faith In America published an ad in the Greensboro newspaper to challenge the anti-gay teachings of the Southern Baptists.

INDIANAPOLIS, INDIANA:

At the invitation of Faith In America, Inc., the Metropolitan Community Churches and Jesus Metropolitan Community Church in Indianapolis collaborated in a media campaign in May and June of 2006. In the Sunday editions of the Indianapolis Star, Faith In America published ads for four weeks that challenged religion-based bigotry. The ads were created and paid for by Faith In America, and Jesus MCC was listed on the ads as the sponsor.

Polling was done before and after the campaign. In answer to the question, "Are you more accepting of homosexuals than you were six months ago?" **16% said yes!**

Faith In America will continue working in Indianapolis with Jesus MCC and the Metropolitan Community Churches. Round 2 of this campaign (April and May, 2007) focused on biblical issues and round 3 (June and July, 2007) returned to the discussion of the history of religion-based bigotry.

COLORADO SPRINGS, COLORADO

A bastion of the Christian Right and Christian Fundamentalism in America (home of James Dobson and his Focus on the Family organization, as well as the Reverend Ted Haggard, former pastor of the New Life Church and former president of the National Association of Evangelicals), Colorado Springs offered a formidable challenge for Faith In America. Our goal was to challenge a targeted evangelical Christian population to critically examine the religious teachings that shape their attitudes toward gay people and, consequently, become more accepting of gay people.

Mitchell Gold and Jimmy Creech visited Colorado Springs and met with a core of progressive religious people who were eager for Faith in America to initiate a campaign that had the potential to change the anti-gay environment there. On two return trips, Jimmy met with a group of clergy and local leaders who were willing to work with Faith In America. The direct-mail campaign, which began the week of November 12, 2006, consisted of four letters– one per week for four weeks, mailed to 16,000 households (identified as evangelical Christians) in Colorado Springs.

Each letter presented a particular perspective: letter #1 – an evangelical Christian writes about his change of heart and mind and how he became accepting of gay people; letter #2 – a lesbian (from Colorado Springs) reflects upon the pain she and others experienced because of religion-based bigotry; letter #3 – Colorado Springs clergy describe how they studied the Bible and church tradition and came to the conclusion that homosexuality is not a sin and who now welcome gay people into their congregations; and finally, letter #4 – Jimmy Creech describes the history of religion-based bigotry and how it is hurting lesbian, gay, bisexual and transgender people today. Each letter concludes with an appeal to end religion-based bigotry now. The final letter includes information about Faith In America as a resource with an invitation to respond via email and letters.

THE 2007 5-CITY CAMPAIGN

Faith In America, Inc. will initiate media and grassroots organizing campaigns in five cities across the United States in 2007. The cities were selected for several reasons, including:

1 allied local and national organizations (i.e., Metropolitan Community Churches, Soulforce, PFLAG, NBJC, NGLTF, GLAAD.) with which we will collaborate;
2 key presidential primary in the states where they are located;
3 they have strong evangelical Christian constituencies; and,
4 they represent middle America.

The five cities are:
Ames, Iowa
Colorado Springs, Colorado
Greenville, South Carolina
Manchester, New Hampshire
Reno, Nevada

Objectives:

1 Create robust dialogue about the misuse of religion teachings which results in discrimination and oppression against gay, lesbian, bisexual and transgender people.
2 Demonstrate to religious-minded people how misguided religious teachings have been used in the past to discriminate against minorities and today those forms of religion-based bigotry are accepted as wrong and antithetical to authentic religious teaching.
3 Provide open-minded clergy and acceptance-minded people of faith a forum to express their disagreement with religion-based bigotry.

Campaign Schedule:

1 Ames IA (March – April)
2 Reno NV (April – May)
3 Manchester NH (August – September)
4 Greenville SC (September – October)
5 Colorado Springs CO (October – November)

- Eight weeks will be devoted to each city with overlapping time frames (organizing for the subsequent campaign will begin in the second city once the campaign is well underway in the first city).
- The initial four weeks will be devoted to grassroots organizing, and meeting with civic and religious leaders. Media-campaigns will last four to six weeks.
- Neighborhood canvassing and Town Hall community meetings will be included at each locale.

Campaign Action strategies:

1 Run four-week direct-mail, radio, newspaper and billboard campaigns in each city.
2 Identify local LGBT organizations and allies in each community and communicate purpose and objectives of campaign.
3 Identify gay-accepting clergy and churches in each community and organize involvement in campaigns.
4 Organize 20 to 50 volunteers to write letters and op-eds to local newspapers to voice opposition to religion-based bigotry against LGBT people.
5 Establish newspaper, radio and TV news contacts in each community and provide story ideas that coincide with campaign.
6 Conduct town hall meetings in each community at end of ad campaigns to educate people about the harm caused by

REV. DR. CINDI LOVE

religion-based bigotry against LGBT people.

7 Conduct extensive polling and research prior to and following each campaign with the assistance of the Gill Foundation.

8 Create a base group of clergy, allies and LGBT leaders in each community for ongoing dialogue and support for those people who have been harmed by religion-based bigotry and for those working to end it.

Outcomes:

1 Create a dialogue vehicle (such as a Town Hall meeting) in each of the five cities to promote the acceptance of LGBT individuals as valued members of society.

2 Provide training in each city to 60+ volunteers who through a 4-week canvassing project in each locale can effectively communicate a strong challenge to religion-based discrimination (names of the trained volunteers will be shared with allied national organizations).

3 Identify new allies and expand the grassroots gay advocacy network in each city which will create a louder voice for pro-LGBT faith organizations.

4 Meet with and develop a network of Welcoming and Affirming clergy.

5 Increase by 25% the number of Welcoming and Affirming congregations in each city.

6 Create a platform for ongoing dialogue among Welcoming and Affirming congregations, clergy and local LGBT organizations.

7 Develop relationships with evangelical Christians, clergy and laypeople.

8 Promote the understanding of and respect for LGBT people to a large number of evangelical Christians in each community.

9 Increase the "more accepting" response 4-6 percent in the post-campaign poll.

10 Promote collateral national media coverage about the campaigns and their successes.

11 Increase awareness in each community of the harm caused by religion-based bigotry.

12 Volunteers recruited in each community will write letters to newspaper that will provide an opposing voice to religion-based discrimination.

13 Door-to-door canvassing material which will provide the opportunity to identify evangelical Christians who opposed religion-based discrimination against LGBT people.

14 Empower nongay Christians to speak out against religious teachings being misused to condemn and discriminate against gay, lesbian, bisexual and transgender individuals.

15 Religious leaders will be less likely to include anti-gay language in Sunday morning sermons and Sunday School teachers will be less likely to use antigay material in lessons.

16 Increase the number of evangelical Christians who no longer view homosexuality as a sin.

17 Less polarization within the faith community on LGBT issues.

18 By increasing the level of respect and understanding among faith communities, people will be less likely to cast ballots against gay equality measures.

Measurables:

1 Large number of letters-to-editor will appear in local newspapers in each community that promote respect and understanding of LGBT people among the faith community.

2 Hateful letters and email responses from communities will be collected to document attitudes promoted by misguided religious teachings.

3 At least four local/regional news articles about each campaign with one article in each locale on local clergy opposed to religion-based bigotry; one article from an LGBT person talking about harm caused by religion-based discrimination; and one article that highlights an evangelical Christian opposed to religion-based discrimination against LGBT individuals.

4 All news articles and letters to the editor will be collected and disseminated via the website.

5 269,000 newspaper readers will be challenged to think about why religion-based discrimination against LGBT individuals is wrong.

6 One person or more in each of 303,000+ households will be challenged to think about how religion is misused to discriminate against LGBT people.

7 Canvassers will document positive responses and obtain names from people who say they oppose religion-based discrimination against LGBT people.

8 All Faith In America email responses and web site traffic from each location will be recorded.

9 Web page for evangelical Christians who disagree with religious-based discrimination will be created and monitored for traffic from each location.

10 Number of attendees at town hall meeting will be documented and forums will be video-taped.

11 Names of attendees at each town hall meetings will be recorded.

12 News coverage in each location of town hall meetings will be documented and disseminated via website.

13 A new gay/straight faith alliance support group forums will be established in each of the five cities for ongoing faith-based dialogue among LGBT individuals and organizations, Welcome and Affirming clergy and new nongay allies.

14 A total of 150,000+ households in the five cities will be polled by telephone prior to each campaign and afterward.
15 Post-campaign polling analyzed for positive shift in level of respect for and acceptance of the LGBT community.

THE 2007 5-CITY CAMPAIGN BUDGET:

Ames IA, pop. 52,000 (18,085 households)

$10,248 four-week newspaper runs in the Ames Tribune (circ. 14,000)

$39,000 mailing (16,000 pc. x 3)

$5,000 (4,000 door hangers w/distribution) (5 canvassers at $400 per day for 5 days plus mileage)

$7,000 movie theaters, 1,000 yard signs, 2,500 bumper stickers

$12,230 radio (8 one-minute spots per day x 20 days) (KHKI Country and Talk)

$30,000 polling

Total: **$103,478**

Colorado Springs CO, pop. 369,000 (141,516 households)

$63,336 four-week newspaper runs Colorado Springs Gazette (circ. 75,000)

$177,000 mailing (125,000 pc. x 3)

$28,000 (30,000 door hangers w/distribution) (30 canvassers at $2,400 per day for 10 days plus mileage)

$24,000 outdoor advertising

$24,000 radio (KKMG KVOR) (4 one-minute spots per day x 20 days)

$30,000 polling

Total: **$346,336**

Greenville SC, pop. 56,000 (24,000 households) (Note: metro area population is around 300,000)

$53,317 four-week newspaper runs Greenville News (circ. 115,000)

$44,000 mailing (22,000 pc. 3 times)

$15,000 outdoor advertising

$11,000 (10,000 door hangers w/distribution) (6 canvassers at $480 per day for 10 days plus mileage)

$22,000 radio (10 one-minute spots per day x 20 days)

$30,000 polling

Total: $175,317

Manchester NH, pop. 110,000 (44,247 households)

$18,300 four-week newspaper runs Union Leader (circ. 85,000)

$84,000 mailing (40,000 pc. 3 times)

$10,000 (9,000 door hangers w/distribution) (8 canvassers at $640 per day x 10 days plus mileage)

$15,000 outdoor advertising

$12,000 radio (WGIR, WZID) (4 one-minute spots per day x 20 days)

$30,000 polling

Total: $169,300

Reno NV, pop. 207,000 (73,904 households)

$44,579 four-week newspaper runs Reno Gazette (circulation 50,000)

$117,000 mailing (66,000 pc. 3x)

$10,000 (8,000 door hangers w/distribution) (10 canvassers at $800 per day for 10 days plus mileage)

$22,000 outdoor advertising

$12,000 radio (Magic 95.5, KBUL Country) (4 one-minute

spots per day x 20 days)
$30,000 polling
Total: $235,579

Staff and travel:

$50,000 stipends for organizers in each city
$25,000 administrative costs in each city
Total: $75,000

Inform Inc.:

Production of door hangers, radio ads and mailings $11,000
Media plan implementation and coordination $12,500
Production coordination $9,000
Assist supervision of organizers/staffers in each locale $5,100
Travel to communities $8,000
Total: $45,600

Additional costs:

$11,000 mailing and phone databases
$45,000 office space, phone, computer, cell phones, utilities for each locale
$11,000 five town meetings event (facility rental, sound and video technician)
Total: $67,000
Total 5-City Campaign budget: $1,217,610

Appendix III

The Daystar Television Network

I pray for Joni Lamb every day. I believe she is a truly anointed minister of the Gospel and she brings much good to the world. Imagine the blessings that she could impart if she were to convert her rhetoric about the "sin of homosexuality" into an affirming message of sisterhood with all God's children.

The Daystar Television Network, headquartered in Bedford, Texas in the greater Dallas/Ft Worth Metroplex and the world's 2nd largest Christian television network, was founded by the husband-and-wife team of Marcus D. and Joni Lamb. He is President and Chief Executive Officer; she is Vice-President and Executive Producer. Daystar's business entity is Word of God Fellowship, Inc., a Georgia-based 501(c) 3 non-profit organization.

Marcus Lamb was raised in Macon, GA and began preaching at age 15. By age 19 Marcus had graduated Magna Cum Laude from Lee College. In 1982, Marcus and Joni Trammell, of Greenville, South Carolina, married and the couple began traveling and ministering in churches in over 20 states. In 1984, they moved to Montgomery, Alabama to build WMCF-TV 45. In 1985, channel 45 became the first full-power Christian television station in the state. At age 27, Marcus was the youngest person ever to build a television station in the United States, and the Lambs quickly gained recognition as "a new breed of televangelists," in the words of one of CBS News anchor. In 1990, they moved to Dallas, Texas to build a new Christian television station. KMPX-TV 29 hit the airwaves in 1993 in the Dallas/Fort Worth area, a market of over 4-million people.

The Daystar Television Network was officially launched on New Year's Eve 1997 with a "live" broadcast featuring Bishop T.D. Jakes from the Potter's House in Dallas. Since then, the Daystar Television Network has emerged as the fastest growing Christian television network in the world. Daystar operates over 50 television stations in major markets across the United States with production facilities in Dallas, Houston, and Denver. In March of 2003, Daystar launched on the HotBird 6 Satellite broadcasting into 74 countries, and on Thaicom 3 broadcasting into 59 countries internationally. Daystar can also be viewed on international satellites including AMC-4, NSS 806, PAS-10, BSkyB, VIASAT and OPTUS B-3, covering the entire footprint of the world reaching over 200 countries.

Daystar has a potential audience of over 128 million viewers in the US alone, which includes 60 million cable and satellite homes. The Network owns and/or operates broadcast television stations in:

Apex NC	Jackson MS	Philadelphia PA
Atlanta GA	Kansas City MO	Phoenix AZ

Birmingham AL	Knoxville TX	Portland ME
Boston MA	Las Vegas NV	Raleigh NC
Buffalo NY	Little Rock AR	Richmond VA
Charleston WV	**Macon GA**	Sacramento CA
Charlotte NC	**Maui HI**	San Antonio TX
Cleveland OH	Memphis TN	San Francisco CA
Dallas TX	**Modesto CA**	St. Louis MO
Denver CO	Montgomery AL	Stockton CA
Gainesville GA	**Montreal QC**	Tampa FL
Honolulu HI	Nashville TN	Tucson AZ
Houston TX	Oklahoma City OK	Tulsa OK
Indianapolis IN	Orlando FL	Washington DC

The network can be seen on DirecTV, affiliated stations, various cable systems, and on the Internet.

Metropolitan Community Church has a congregation or an affiliate in every city where Daystar Television Network owns or operates except the ones listed above in bold face type. Perhaps you would like to help us start a study group in those places? If not, make sure you wear a WJD t-shirt.

Notes

AUTHOR'S NOTE (PAGES 15–21)

ENDNOTES

1 Jesus MCC's website is http://www.jesusmcc.org.
2 Faith In America's website is http://www.faithinamerica.com.
3 Metropolitan Community Churches website is http://www.mcchurch.org.
4 Margaret Mead. *Continuities in Cultural Evolution,* Transaction Publishers, June 1999.
5 Everett M. Rogers has produced a considerable body of work;

the sources I've used mort frequently are his book *Diffusion of Innovation*, The Free Press, New York, 1962, and the article "New Product Adoption and Diffusion," *Journal of Consumer Research: An Interdisciplinary Quarterly*, vol. 2, issue 4, pp. 290 – 301.

6 Vijay Mahajan, Eitan Muller and Frank Bass; "Diffusion of New Products: Empirical Generalizations and Managerial Uses," *Marketing Science*, Special issue on Empirical Generalizations in Marketing, 1995, Vol. 14, No 3, Part 2 of 2, G79 – G88.

7 The firm's website is http://www.publicpolicypolling.com.

8 When I use the term "Christian Right" I am referring to the broad and varied political movement of Christian social conservatives, principally in the USA, that coalesced in the 1970s and has grown to include millions of Americans and myriad organizations, institutions, media enterprises, leaders, elected officials, and special projects. The Christian Right transcends denominational lines, but very generally it can be said that most of its members ascribe to conservative evangelicalism. The movement comprises a number of influence threads including, but not limited to, Christian fundamentalism, Pentecostalism, conservative Protestant theological movements and conservative movements within Roman Catholicism. A great majority of the Christian Right's membership believe that the United States was founded as a Christian nation. Because of that viewpoint, they see their efforts as a Christian reclamation of American society.

9 Job 27: 2 – 6.

10 Jeremiah 21: 12.

11 Peter Hellman, *When Courage Was Stronger Than Fear*, MJF Books, 1980, p. xiii.

12 Both Matthew Shepard and Sean Kennedy were murdered in hate crimes; they died in October 1998 and May 2007, respectively. See http://en.wikipedia.org/wiki/Matthew_

Shepard and http://en.wikipedia.org/wiki/Sean_W._Kennedy for more information.

13 Message retrieved from the voice-mailbox of the MCC toll-free number, 1 866 HOPE MCC. Transcribed by Frank Zerilli.

14 See http://napsterization.org/stories/archives/000513.html for a post and comments related to assessing the extent of bloggers' reach and influence.

Chapter 1

15 Dr. Spencer Johnson, *Who Moved My Cheese?*, 2006, Spencer Johnson Partners. All rights reserved.

16 Dr. Johnson's website is http://www.spencerjohnson.com/whomovedmycheese/phenomenon.php.

17 Information taken from Dr. Johnson's website.

18 Matthew 25: 45.

19 Bishop Carlton Pearson, *The Gospel of Inclusion*, Azusa Press/Council Oak Books, April 2007, p. 49. Used by permission.

20 Walter Bagehot, *Physics and Politics*, Ivan R. Dee, Publisher, April 1999. Used by permission.

21 Garry Wills, *What Jesus Meant*, Penguin (Non-Classics), Feb 2007, p. 27. Used by permission.

Chapter 2

22 Micah 6: 8.

23 Chris Bull & John Gallagher, *Perfect Enemies: The Religious right, the Gay Movement and the Politics of the 1990s*, Crown Publishing Group, New York, NY, USA, 1996.

24 National Faith Spokesperson Training, GLAAD's National News and Religion Faith & Values Programs, December, 2007. (GLAAD is the acronym for Gay & Lesbian Alliance Against Defamation; their website is http://www.glaad.org/)

25 The Barna Group, "Annual Barna Group Survey Describes Changes in America's Religious Beliefs and Practices," April 11, 2005, The Barna Update, http://www.barna.org.

26 The Rev. Dr. King delivered his speech, "I Have a Dream," at the Lincoln Memorial in Washington DC, on August 28, 1963.

27 http://www.worldofquotes.com/topic/Affection/index.html.

Chapter 3

28 Rogers' work had been widely studied, analyzed and written about. I found the information in an unnamed graduate student's paper particularly helpful. http://www.tcw.utwente.nl/theorieenoverzicht/Theory%20clusters/Communication%20and%20Information%20Technology/Diffusion_of_Innovations_Theory.doc.

29 Although there is no uniformly accepted use of the term, "Millennial Generation" is used here to mean individuals born in the years 1979–2001. According to the 2006 Cone Millennial Cause Study, 61% of the cohort feels personally responsible for making a difference in the world. http://www.coneinc.com/oldsite/Pages/pr_45.html.

30 Malcolm Gladwell, *The Tipping Point: How Little Things Can Make a Big Difference*, Little Brown, 2000.

31 Growth does not appear everywhere at the same time, but rather becomes manifest, with variable intensity, at points or poles of growth.

Chapter 4

32 The Task Force's website is http://www.thetaskforce.org.

33 The Human Rights Campaign's website is http://www.hrc.org.

34 As a "thank you" for their involvement, all participants were sent a copy of the DVD "Mortal Tongues Awake" developed

by Patricia Mathis, who served as Deputy Assistant Secretary of the Treasury under President Jimmy Carter.

35 Barbara Delaney, the CEO of Navratilova, Inc., was with us at the Town Hall Meeting. Both Barbara and Martina Navratilova have continued to be great supporters of MCC through our conferences and events. We are very grateful for their assistance.

36 Information taken from statements by Rev. Jeff Miner in his 2006 report to the *Would Discriminate? Campaign* Team.

37 The *Indianapolis Star* ran a story by staff reporter Robert King which featured a photograph of one of the defaced billboards and quotes from Rev. Jeff Miner and other area ministers. The website http://advanceindiana.blogspot.com/2007/04/billboard-promoting-tolerance-defaced.html is one of many at which you can view the photo, read parts of the article and/or find comments thereon.

38 Clear Channel's website is http://www.clearchannel.com.

Chapter 5

39 The creation of the unique webpage, www.agcmcc.org/wjd, was a part of their campaign.

40 Language taken from HRC's website.

41 Language taken from NGLTF's website.

42 You can read more about and see images from the 2007 Clergy Call for Justice and Equality in the Religion & Faith pages of the HRC website, http://www.hrc.org.

43 Rob Bell, *Velvet Elvis: Repainting the Christian Faith*, Zondervan, 2005, p. 13.

44 "Tearing Down Walls, Building Up Hope." is the official slogan of Metropolitan Community Churches.

45 The National Gay and Lesbian Task Force, "Survey of Denominations by the National Gay and Lesbian Task

Force," 2005.

46 http://www.jesusmcc.org/go/wouldjesus.html; used by permission.

Chapter 6

47 Some of the details of Brent's story can be found at the Faith in America website, http://www.faithinamerica.com. I appreciate his willingness to share his experiences.

48 Brent Childers now works for Faith in America and speaks up with skill and conviction.

49 More details about the Bishops and Elders Council and this particular meeting can be found at http://www.welcomingresources.org/bishopsandelders06.htm.

50 This and the previous two quotes are all from Jack Rogers' book *Jesus, the Bible, and Homosexuality*, Westminster John Knox Press, 2006, pages ix – 15, and are used with the author's permission.

Chapter 7

51 Rev. Jeff Miner and John Tyler Connoley, *The Children are Free*, Jesus Metropolitan Community Church, 2002.

52 John 8: 31 – 32

53 See a letter of apology from the Episcopal House of Bishops at http://www.episcopalchurch.org/3577_73047_ENG_HTM.htm.

54 From the Southern Baptist Conventions website, http://www.sbc.net/resolutions/amResolution.asp?ID=984.

55 Jack Rogers, *Jesus, The Bible and Homosexuality*, p. 34.

56 Rodney Stark, "A civil religion: how Christianity created free and prosperous societies." *The American Enterprise*, May 2006, p. 17. Reprinted with the permission of the author and

the American Enterprise Institute for Public Policy Research, Washington DC.

57 Tom Heneghan, Religion Editor, Reuters UK, http://uk.reuters.com/article/reutersEdge/idUKNOA83516120070418, April 2007.

58 Specifically, you might want to read *The Children are Free*, already referenced earlier in these notes. The book is available through both Amazon.com and Barnes&Noble.com and may be available elsewhere, as well.

59 http://www.jesusmcc.org/news/archives/5.

60 Oliver "Buzz" Thomas, "When religion loses its credibility" *USAToday*, Nov 20, 2006, http://blogs.usatoday.com/oped2006/11/when_religion_1htm. Used with the author's permission.

61 José Comblin, *The Holy Spirit and Liberation*, translated from the Portuguese by Paul Burns, Maryknoll, New York: Orbis Books, 1989.

62 Melanie Martinez, "Interpretations of the Christian Message," an unpublished work, March 2007. Used with the author's permission.

Chapter 8

63 The excerpts included here are reproduced with their original syntax, grammar, etc. intact. You can read this discussion thread in its entirety at http://www.churchmarketingsucks.com/archives/2006/06would_jesus_dis.html.

Chapter 9

64 A dear friend of mine, Rev. Elder Lillie Brock, is the co-author, along with Mary Ann Salerno, of *The Change Cycle: The Secret to Getting Through Life's Difficult Changes*, (Bridge Builder Media, 1994) which explores this resistance to change. In

recent years, her work has greatly informed my understanding of what it takes to encourage people through the stages of change necessary for the adoption of new technology or ideas. Unfortunately, I did not have the benefit of her text until a few years ago or I might have wasted less time getting to where I am today. I recommend her book as an excellent primer for dealing with either personal or professional changes.

65 You can read more information about the Birthing of Giants program on Inc.'s website, at http://www.inc.com/events/birthingofgiants/.

66 I was still at the TORO Company when I began working towards ordination. As you can imagine, I didn't talk much about it in the halls of TORO, but there were good people there, including the former Chairman of the Board, Kenneth Melrose and Chuck Lounsbury, one of the company's former Presidents, who were very supportive of me. They believed in a strong corporate culture where all people (even a woman from West Texas) had a chance give their best.

67 Galatians 3: 28.

Chapter 10

68 Information from the ChristianityToday.com website, http://www.christianitytoday.com/movies/interviews/peterlalonde.html.

69 From an article on the Spero News website, http://www.speroforum.com/site/print.asp?idarticle=1773.

70 Mark 2: 16.

Chapter 11

71 Statistic quoted by Dr. Paul Ray in his address at the Sacred Activism Conference in Tulsa OK, May 9, 2007.

72 FOX's website is http://www.fox.com.

73 This incident was widely reported in the days following the attack. One of the accounts can be perused at http://www.thedenverchannel.com/news/11608272/detail.html.

74 Information from the website of The Interfaith Alliance, http://www.interfaithalliance.org/elections.

75 All of the organizations listed are politically active and communicate regularly with elected officials.

76 Dr. Paul Ray, from his address in Tulsa OK, cited earlier.

77 This is as close as I'll come to writing about the particularities of my faith. This book is certainly not intended to be proselytizing in any way.

Chapter 12

78 From the website of the US Department of Justice, http://www.ojp.usdoj.gov/bjs/pub/pdf/hcrvp.pdf.

79 From the Southern Poverty Law Center's website, http://wwwsplcenter.org/intel/news/item.jsp?site_area=1&aid=145.

Chapter 13

80 I grew up, and now reside again, in Abilene, Texas; one of the ten most conservative cities in the US I love my hometown, but it has an Achilles' Heel in the form of religiously based bigotry that is sanctioned by the local city government.

81 In 1952 a bill proclaiming an annual *National Day of Prayer* was passed unanimously by both houses of Congress. President Truman signed the bill into law and in 1988 the observance was fixed on the first Thursday of May each year. Until 1998 the NDP events were generally promoted as multi-faith proceedings, but since then have come to be increasingly dominated by the Christian Right.

82 Although the designation "Official Website" has since been removed from the NDP Task Force website (www.ndptf.org) a copy of the graphics current in early May of 2007 can be viewed at http://www.jewsonfirst.org/07b/national_prayer_day.html. Numerous other references dating to the spring of 2007 and containing the language "National Day of Prayer Official Website" in relation to the NDP Task Force site can be found with a straightforward internet search.

83 From page 56 of "the national day of prayer task force Resource Manual" which can be viewed at http://media1.ssiwt.com/ndptf/downloads/Resource%20ManualUpdated.pdf.

84 Excerpts from Mr. Foxman's address can be read at http://www.adl.org/Religious_Freedom/religion_public_square.asp.

85 Chip Berlet, "Human rights, dignity, and Spiritual Belief," November 21, 2005. http://www.talk2action.org/story/2005/11/21/123810/82. Used with the author's permission.

86 The Joni show aired "Love in the House" in 2004.

87 Exodus International is an organization founded some 30 years ago with the stated purpose of "freeing" affected persons from homosexuality.

88 National Gay and Lesbian Task Force, *Youth in the Crosshairs: the Third Wave of Ex-Gay Activism*, Task Force Policy Institute, NGLTF, March 2006. http://www.thetaskforce.org/press/releases/pr923_030206.

89 An internet search using the keywords "anti-gay violence" and either "Jamaica" or "Eastern Europe" can prove eye-opening.

Appendix I

90 Dr. Trichy Krishnan is Head of the Marketing Department at the National University of Singapore (NUS). He is a Mechanical engineer with a Ph.D. in Marketing Management Science from the University of Texas, Dallas. Dr. Krishnan has

over 10 years experience in developing math models for sales and pricing forecasts while working at NUS and previously with Rice University.

Printed in the United States
109562LV00002B/283-285/P

9 781425 172886